The McCall's

Book of Rugmaking

BY THE EDITORS OF McCALL'S

NEEDLEWORK & CRAFTS

PUBLICATIONS

Simon and Schuster/ The McCall Pattern Company   New York

Copyright © 1959, 1963, 1968, 1970, 1971, 1972,
1974, 1975, 1976 by The McCall Pattern Company

Published by Simon and Schuster
A Gulf+Western Company
Rockefeller Center, 630 Fifth Avenue
New York, New York 10020

Designed by Jill Weber

Manufactured in the United States of America

1 2 3 4 5 6 7 8 9 10

Library of Congress Cataloging in Publication Data

The McCall's book of rugmaking.
1. Rugs. I. McCall's needlework and crafts.
II. Title: Book of rugmaking.
TT850.M32 1976 746.7 75-43857
ISBN 0-671-22205-8

Contents

Foreword

Anyone can make a rug! To show you how, the editors of *McCall's Needlework & Crafts* magazine have assembled in one book over fifty rugs in nine fascinating techniques—complete with color illustrations, patterns, and instructions to guide you every step of the way. With a wide variety of styles to choose from, including Victorian florals, Art Deco geometrics, Contemporary abstracts and more, you will find the one perfect rug design suited to your own tastes and talents.

The book begins with three ways of making pile rugs. The oldest method is hand hooking, in which fabric loops are fixed in a burlap backing with a simple tool, for a lovely shaded rose or a series of rectangular tiles. Next are two modern adaptations of the hand hook that use yarn to make the pile: the punch needle on fabric and the latch hook on canvas. Still other rugs are tufted with a yarn needle, such as the radiant Scandinavian ryas and the soft boudoir rugs knotted on a filet-mesh base, to knit or crochet.

The old-favorite method of making a flat-surface rug consists of braiding fabric strips into simple but effective patterns; principal tools are your hands.

Perhaps no technique offers more versatility than needlepoint. Patterns here range from strawberries or thistles worked on fine canvas in an interesting herringbone stitch to the panorama of "Nature's Kingdom" in large-mesh quick point. The woven rugs include an authentic Navajo mat to work on a simple frame loom and a dramatic rib-weave harvest sun. A felt rug appliquéd with giant Hawaiian-style cutouts can be stitched up by anyone with a sewing machine.

A final chapter offers valuable technical suggestions for finishing your rug, along with hints on designing, joining canvas, enlarging designs, and much more!

1

Hand-Hooked Rugs

The American tradition of hand hooking seems to derive from early Scandinavians, who hooked clothing and coverlets. They introduced hooking to the Britons, and the Pilgrims brought it to America. The settlers first made coverings for the bed, and later for the floor. We still make many of our rugs the same way—looping strips of fabric through a backing with a hand hook.

general directions

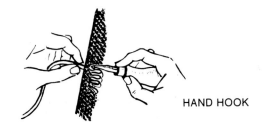

HAND HOOK

MATERIALS AND EQUIPMENT: The hand hook for rugmaking resembles a large steel crochet needle embedded in a wooden handle. Firmly woven burlap about 40″ wide is the usual foundation fabric; old burlap bags are often used. There are also cotton and linen foundation fabrics, called warp cloth, that are woven with a somewhat open mesh, allowing the needle to slip in easily. If foundation fabric is not large enough, it can be pieced by lapping one piece of fabric over the other about two inches and running a line of catch-stitching down both edges. Designs must be shown on the top (right) side of the fabric, since work is done from the top. Although you may be able to hook with the fabric in your lap, most hookers find it easier to stretch it on a rug hoop or frame (see page 163).

Hand-hooked rugs are usually made from fabric strips cut from old clothing or blankets, although new fabric may be used to supplement this, or even to make an entire rug. Try to use material of the same weight, thickness, and fiber content for the whole rug so that it will wear evenly. Wool wears very well and does not show soil as much as silk, rayon, or cotton. Stocking or necktie strips may be used as highlights in wool rugs or to hook small ornamental mats.

If you wish to make your rug washable, it is important that the material be absolutely colorfast. New or old, all material should be washed in hot water and borax to loosen and remove any excess dye. Wash each color separately, then rinse until no more dye comes out. (If the material is soiled, use naphtha soap.) Do not wring; hang in the sun to dry. The colors will not seem faded when hooked, because color is relative and depends upon placement of adjacent colors for the overall effect.

To obtain the desired colors, you can dye your fabrics yourself (see page 166). Lovely color effects can be obtained by shading areas. A group of shaded colors for making a motif is known as a "swatch" and is made of five or six 3″ x 12″ pieces of fabric that shade from light to dark in the same hue. Swatches may be purchased at art needlework departments, from rug designers, or may be prepared at home. (We describe how to prepare material in related tones of a color in the directions for dyeing on page 166.) Interesting effects are also achieved by mixing materials to include tweeds, herringbone weaves, flannels, and twills. The shadings add variety of tone and make the rug more practical—a slightly variegated background shows less soil. Mingling of color is called "wiggling in."

Estimating Amount of Material: Use the general rule that ½ lb. of fabric will cover 1 sq. ft. of backing; or, 1½ to 2 sq. yds. of wool or 2 sq. yds. of cotton will hook about 1 sq. ft.

CUTTING INTO STRIPS: The width of strips varies according to the thickness of the material. Strips of the same fabric should be cut in uniform widths, although strips to be used for fine detail in a small section may be cut narrower. A machine that cuts strips evenly is sold in needlework departments and by mail. Most strips are cut on the straight of the goods, but some people prefer them cut slightly on the bias for more give. Fabric should be cut as narrowly as the weave allows. Closely woven fabric such as flannel is cut in strips as narrow as 1/16" to 1/8" wide; more loosely woven fabric is cut from 3/16" to 5/16". Cotton strips should be ¼" to ½".

PREPARING BACKGROUND FABRIC: Before hooking is begun, mark design on fabric (page 165) and plan the finished edge (page 162).

HOOKING: Hand hooking is a simple method of putting loops of narrow strips of fabric through meshes (between threads) of background fabric. If you have never hooked before, practice on a small area outside the rug design. Hold the hook above the foundation fabric in the right hand; hold the fabric strip underneath with the left. Push the hook through the fabric and draw a loop up through to the desired height; then reinsert the hook in the fabric close by and pull up another loop. Give hook a little clockwise twist as you pull the loops through. This makes a firmer and longer wearing pile. Care must be taken to have all loops the same height; height is determined by the fabric used and the width of strip. If loops are to be cut, they should be no longer than usual. For fine hooking, loops are pulled through the mesh about 3/16"; for coarser hooking, pull the loops approximately ¼" high. You will gauge how far apart your stitches should be by the width or thickness of the strands and the height of the loops; they should be close enough together to stay in place, yet far enough apart so that the rug will not buckle. Continue inserting hook through burlap and pulling up loops. Do as much of one color as possible at one time. Pull ends through to top when starting and ending a strand; clip ends even with loops.

Usually the design part of the rug is worked before the background, and the portion of design that appears in "front" or "on top" (the shape that appears in front of the adjoining shapes) is worked first in order to keep the shapes from being lost. To obtain an interesting background texture, do not work in straight lines. Fill in background around the motifs, then continue to keep direction of lines irregular. If you are working the rug in a small frame, work all motifs and background before rolling to new section.

DAMASK ROSE RUG

Damask roses in shaded pinks and reds and framed in deep-toned scrolls are reminiscent of traditional hand-hooked rug designs. Included are patterns for dimensional color shading.

Rug courtesy of Rebecca Andrews

SIZE: About 30″ x 49″.

EQUIPMENT: Hand hook. Large needle. Scissors. Ruler. Soft pencil. Paper for patterns. Tracing paper. Rug frame (optional). Dressmaker's tracing (carbon) paper. Blunt instrument (such as dry ballpoint pen) for transferring designs.

MATERIALS: Wool fabrics in the following colors: small amounts of six blending shades through light, medium, and deep pink to medium, dark, and very dark red; five blended shades of blue-green from pale aqua to dark blue-green; five shades of yellow-green from light to dark; approximately 2 lbs. light beige and 2¼ lbs. dark beige. Foundation fabric, 38″ x 57″. Rug binding, 4½ yds. Carpet thread.

DIRECTIONS: Read general directions on page 1.

To Make Patterns: Draw a rectangle 30″ x 49″ on foundation fabric (finished rug will be a little smaller); draw horizontal and vertical center lines as guide for design. Enlarge pattern on page 6 (omitting letters) by copying on paper ruled in 1″ squares; center lines of pattern are indicated by arrows.

Mark pattern on foundation fabric, following directions on page 165; match center lines on fabric with arrows on pattern. Mark complete scroll section shown between arrows in each corner of foundation. Mark right rose motif, plus center leaves and one petal of left rose, then reverse pattern and complete left rose motif.

To Hook Rug: Work rug, following shading charts on pages 4 and 5 and working colors as indicated by numbers and shaded sketches. Numbers run 1, 2, 3, 4, 5, 6—from light to dark. Broken lines indicate direction for working stitches. Letters on pattern indicate placing of colors.

When working center rose A, in six shades from light pink (1) to very dark red (6), note how the gradations are planned to give the flower roundness and form. To keep each part of the flower clearly defined, always work first the shape that appears in front of the adjoining shapes. For example, the curled-over part of the petal appears in front of the rest of the petal. The bowl section is in front of the outer petals. These shapes should be outlined and filled in, shading as indicated. Outline each petal and fill in. Work other rose, leaves, buds, and scrolls. Work background no. 1 in light beige and background no. 2 in dark beige.

Finish binding rug (see directions on page 162).

SCROLLS E

SHADING CHART FOR DAMASK ROSE RUG

ROSES A

LEAVES B

CENTER LEAVES C

LEAVES G

ROSEBUDS D

ROSES A:
1 LIGHT PINK
2 MEDIUM PINK
3 DEEP PINK
4 MEDIUM RED
5 DARK RED
6 VERY DARK RED

LEAVES B:
1 PALE YELLOW-GREEN
2 MEDIUM-LIGHT YELLOW-GREEN
3 MEDIUM YELLOW-GREEN
4 MEDIUM-DARK YELLOW-GREEN
5 DARK YELLOW-GREEN

CENTER LEAVES C:
LEAVES F and G:
SCROLLS E:
1 PALE AQUA
2 MEDIUM AQUA
3 DEEP AQUA
4 MEDIUM BLUE-GREEN
5 DARK BLUE-GREEN

ROSEBUDS D:
3 DEEP PINK
4 MEDIUM RED
5 DARK RED

BACKGROUND 1: LIGHT BEIGE
BACKGROUND 2: DARK BEIGE

ANTIQUE FLORAL RUG

This traditional, hand-hooked rug blends beautifully with any decorating scheme for a pleasing effect year after year.

SIZE: 30″ x 48″.

EQUIPMENT: Hand hook. Large needle. Scissors. Ruler. Soft pencil. Paper for patterns. Tracing paper. Rug frame (optional). Dressmaker's tracing (carbon) paper. Tracing wheel or dry ballpoint pen.

MATERIALS: Foundation fabric, 34″ x 52″. Wool fabrics in following colors and approximate amounts: deep red, 1 lb.; bright red, ½ lb.; deep yellow, ½ lb.; light blue-green, ¼ lb.; medium blue-green, ½ lb.; medium green, ¼ lb.; light yellow-green, ½ lb.; olive green, 1 lb.; black, ½ lb.; beige, 3 lbs.; lavender, ¼ lb. Rug binding, 4½ yds. Carpet thread.

DIRECTIONS: Read general directions on page 1.

To Make Patterns: Trace patterns for center design, oval border, and corners. Mark outline of rug, 30″ x 48″, on burlap. Fold burlap in half crosswise and lengthwise; mark center and middle of each side; open burlap. Place center design, evenly spaced, on burlap and transfer, using carbon paper. Mark an oval on burlap, pointed at each end, with sides of oval 4½″ from marked side of rug, and pointed ends 6½″ from edge of rug. Transfer oval border all around marked oval, repeating the two scrolls so they meet at ends as shown in illustration.

Mark a line 1″ in from edge of rug all around. Transfer corner motif to all four corners.

To Hook Rug: Stitch binding to rug fabric following directions on page 162. Hook flowers, leaves, and scrolls, following color key and numbers on patterns. Shade flowers on dotted lines, if desired. Referring to the photograph, reverse the red and yellow flowers in opposite corners. Make all stems, petal separations, and leaf accents black unless otherwise marked on pattern. Hook outer straight border with three rows of olive. Fill in background with beige.

Finish binding according to directions on page 162.

OVAL BORDER

1 DEEP RED
2 LIGHT RED
3 DEEP YELLOW
4 LIGHT BLUE-GREEN
5 MEDIUM BLUE-GREEN
6 MEDIUM GREEN
7 MEDIUM YELLOW-GREEN
8 OLIVE GREEN
9 LAVENDER
10 BLACK

CORNERS

CENTER DESIGN

1 DEEP RED
2 LIGHT RED
3 DEEP YELLOW
4 LIGHT BLUE-GREEN
5 MEDIUM BLUE-GREEN
6 MEDIUM GREEN
7 MEDIUM YELLOW-GREEN
8 OLIVE GREEN
9 LAVENDER
10 BLACK

VICTORIAN ROSE RUG

An heirloom design to cherish, this beautiful antique-pattern rug is made from wool rags in rich colors. The floral forms are sculptured in bas-relief.

1 ROSE
2 SCARLET
3 BLACK
4 BLUE-GREEN
5 LIGHT GREEN
6 MEDIUM GREEN
7 YELLOW-GREEN MIXTURE
8 GOLDEN BROWN
9 LIGHT BROWN
10 YELLOW
OUTER BACKGROUND—BLACK
INNER BACKGROUND—GOLDEN BROWN

13

SIZE: 27" x 47".

EQUIPMENT: Hand hook. Rug frame (optional). Paper for patterns. Tracing paper. Soft pencil. Dressmaker's tracing (carbon) paper. Blunt instrument (such as dry ballpoint pen) for transferring designs.

MATERIALS: Burlap, 31" x 51". Wool fabrics in the following colors and approximate amounts: golden brown, 2 lbs.; black, 2 lbs.; light brown, 1 lb.; yellow-green mixture (light and medium), 1 lb.; blue-green, ½ lb.; light green, ½ lb.; medium green, ½ lb.; scarlet, ½ lb.; rose, ½ lb.; small amount of yellow. Rug binding. Carpet thread.

DIRECTIONS: Read general directions on page 1.

To Make Patterns: Enlarge patterns on paper ruled to 1" squares. Trace scroll pattern for rug border. Mark outline of rug on burlap, 27" x 47". Fold burlap in half crosswise and mark center line. Following general directions, place pattern with dash line on side scroll at center line and with sides of corner scroll about 1½" from outer marked lines. Trace design onto burlap using carbon paper. Turn pattern over and place on opposite side of center line; trace. Repeat on other two corners to complete scroll border.

Place rose design on one half of burlap with long berry stem crossing center; trace design onto burlap. Turn pattern over and repeat on other half of burlap.

To Hook Rug: Stitch rug binding or stitch around edge of burlap, following directions on page 162. Hook flowers, leaves, and scrolls, using colors indicated on pattern (and following color keys). Work inner background in golden brown; work outer background in black (an interesting mottled effect can be obtained by using different shades of black).

Finish binding according to directions on page 162.

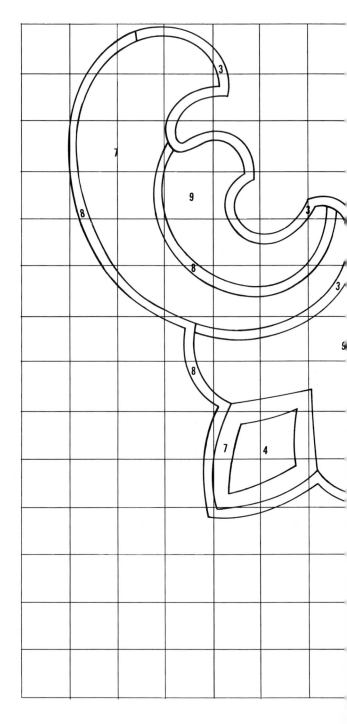

1 ROSE
2 SCARLET
3 BLACK
4 BLUE-GREEN
5 LIGHT GREEN
6 MEDIUM GREEN
7 YELLOW-GREEN MIXTURE
8 GOLDEN BROWN
9 LIGHT BROWN
10 YELLOW
OUTER BACKGROUND—BLACK
INNER BACKGROUND—GOLDEN BROWN

GOURD-AND-LEAF RUG

Reminiscent of Colonial times, graceful gourds and leaves set within a geometric framework make appealing motifs for a rug hooked in mellow colors.

SIZE: 35″ x 69″.

EQUIPMENT: Hand hook. Large needle. Scissors. Paper for patterns. Ruler. Soft pencil. Rug frame (optional). Dressmaker's tracing (carbon) paper. Blunt instrument (such as dry ballpoint pen) for transferring designs.

MATERIALS: Wool fabrics in the following colors and approximate amounts: light gray, 1½ lbs.; medium gray, 1½ lbs.; mixture of dark gray, light gray tweed, and dark gray tweed, 1½ lbs.; mixture of pale peach, medium peach, light orange, light yellow, medium yellow, ¾ lb.; mixture of dark olive green, medium olive green, medium yellow-green, light yellow-green, dark green, medium green, pale green, light blue-green, dark blue-green, 1 lb.; black, ¼ lb.; small amounts of purple, red, and light brown. Burlap, 42″ x 75″. Rug binding, 6 yds. Carpet thread.

DIRECTIONS: To Make Patterns: Enlarge gourd-and-leaf patterns on pages 18–19 by copying on paper ruled in 1″ squares. Mark rectangle 35″ x 69″ on burlap and mark off rectangle in 11½″ squares. Make a diamond inside each square by marking across corners from center of each side of square. Transfer gourds and leaves to center of each square, following directions on page 165 and placing motifs according to chart. Have the tips of leaves and gourds on each half of rug face center line. Reverse some of the leaves.

To Hook Rug: Read general directions on page 1. Sew rug binding to burlap around edge of rug, following directions on page 162. Hook gourds and leaves before working background.

Leaves: All leaf motifs are the same colors except for the tendrils, which may be red or medium orange. Leaf outline is medium olive green; stem may be outlined in dark blue-green and filled in with light blue-green. Veins are one row of purple and one row of brown. Fill in rest of leaf, starting around veins, with dark olive green, shading to medium olive green, medium yellow-green, and light yellow-green.

Gourds 1 and 5: These are the same shape but different colors. Gourd 1 is outlined in light orange, with stem in medium olive green. Work gourd in stripes of pale peach (plain sections on pattern) and medium peach with light orange (speckled sections of pattern). Gourd 5 is outlined in dark blue-green; stem is filled in with brown. Work gourd in stripes of dark, medium, and pale green, except bottom speckled section on pattern. Work bottom in stripes of medium peach and light orange combined, alternating with pale green stripes that extend from top of gourd through bottom section.

Gourds 2 and 6: Both of these have purple outlines, with stems filled in with brown and medium green mixed. For gourd 2, speckled sections of pattern are light gray with a row of medium yellow around them. The bottom third of gourd is filled in with medium yellow; remainder is light yellow. For gourd 6, the speckled areas of pattern are medium yellow with a row of pale green around them. Work a row of medium yellow inside purple outline and a row of pale green inside medium yellow. Fill in remainder with light yellow.

Gourd 3: Work bottom section in stripes of medium olive green (speckled areas of pattern) and medium yellow-green combined with light yellow-green (plain areas of pattern). Top is in stripes of light orange (dash-line areas) and pale and medium peach combined (plain areas). Stem is light blue-green.

Gourds 4 and 9: Outline bottom section and stem of gourd 4 in dark blue-green. Fill in stem with light gray tweed and medium olive green mixed. Bottom section is stripes of dark green worked on lines of pattern and medium and pale green combined (plain areas of pattern). Work top section in stripes of light orange and medium peach combined (speckled areas) and pale peach (plain areas). Gourd 9 is outlined in purple; stem is filled in with brown. Work rest of gourd in stripes of light orange and medium peach combined and pale peach stripes.

Gourd 7: Outline entire gourd in purple; fill stem in with dark blue-green and medium blue-green mixed. Work bottom section in stripes of pale green (plain areas of pattern), medium yellow-green (speckled areas of pattern), and medium olive green (wide black lines of pattern). On top section, work lines in pale green, plain areas of pattern in a combination of pale and medium peach and light orange.

Gourd 8: Outline entire gourd in purple. Work bottom section in stripes of medium peach (speckled areas of pattern) and pale peach (plain areas of pattern). On top section, work a row of light blue-green inside purple outline. Fill in stem with purple and light blue-green mixed. Make lines of pattern light orange. Fill in remainder of top section in medium yellow-green stripes and stripes of light yellow-green and medium yellow-green combined.

Hook two rows of black between squares and around all of the diamonds. Fill in the backgrounds of all the diamonds with light gray; corners of gourd squares with medium gray; corners of leaf squares with diagonal stripes of dark and light gray tweed and dark gray.

Finish binding rug (see directions on page 162).

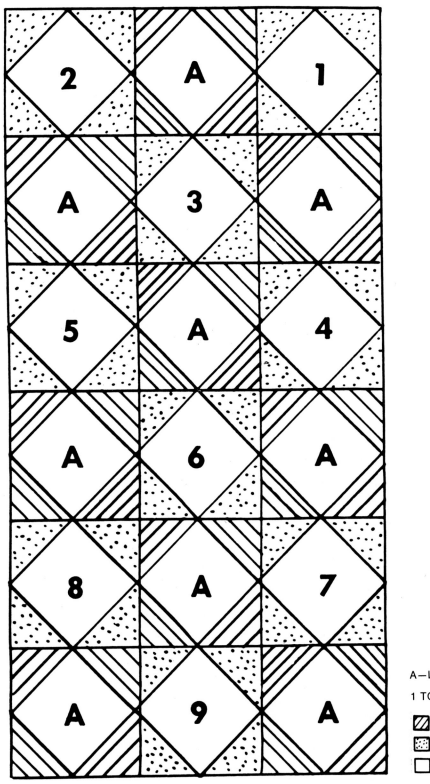

A—LEAVES

1 TO 9—GOURDS

STRIPED

MEDIUM GRAY

LIGHT GRAY

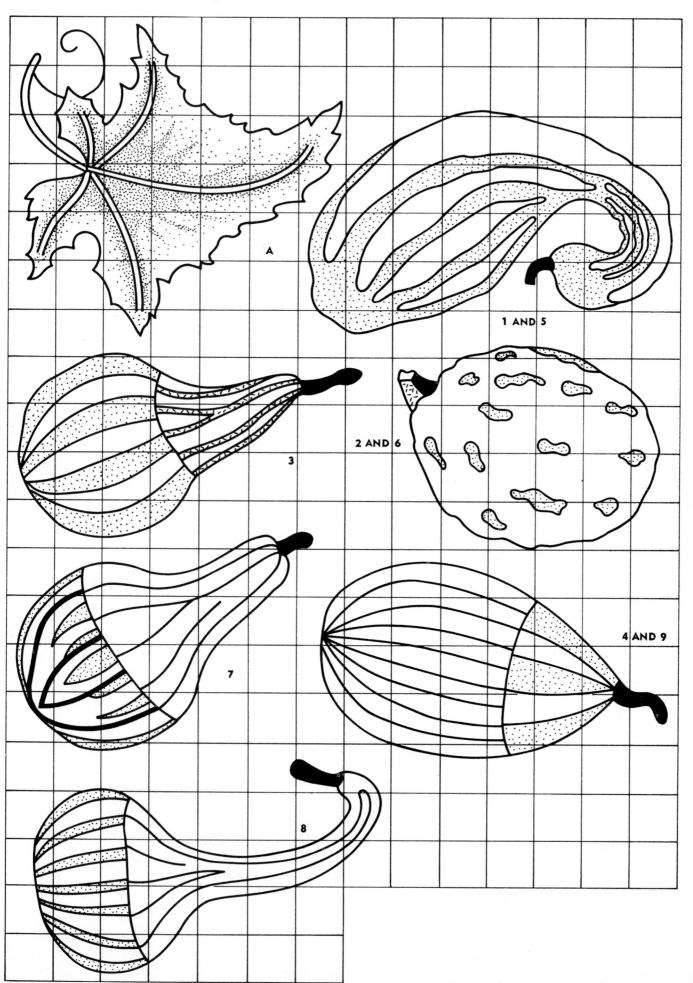

A

1 AND 5

2 AND 6

3

4 AND 9

7

8

19

SHADED TILE RUG

This simple geometric design is hooked in shades of two contrasting colors. The color detail represents a section of the rug in progress.

SIZE: 30″ x 49″.

EQUIPMENT: Hand hook. Large needle. Scissors. Ruler. Soft pencil. Rug frame (optional).

MATERIALS: Wool fabrics in several related shades of two contrasting colors, such as red and green: 2½ lbs. total of each color. Burlap, 40″ wide, 1½ yds. Rug binding, 5 yds. Carpet thread.

DIRECTIONS: Read general directions on page 1. Mark rectangle 30″ x 49″ on burlap and divide into rectangles 3½″ x 6″—five rectangles on width of rug, fourteen on length.

To Hook Rug: Start hooking around outline of one rectangle, using first one shade of red, then another. Work around, inside outline, for two or three rows. Work outlines of adjacent rectangles in green. Fill in red rectangle, being careful to distribute shades for a well-blended effect. Fill in green rectangles as for red rectangles, working adjacent red outlines first.

Finish binding rug; see page 162.

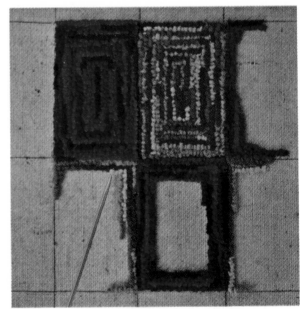

2

Punch-Needle Rugs

The punch needle is a modern type of rug hook that uses yarn instead of fabric strips. The punch needle became popular in America in the 1930s. Several kinds are now available; they all make loops of even length automatically, producing a rug with a soft close pile.

general directions

MATERIALS AND EQUIPMENT: Some yarn companies supply patented punch needles that punch yarn through a foundation fabric to deposit loops of measured height. Some of the more common types of punch needles are used with skeins of wool or cotton rug yarn. There is usually an adjustment on the needle to regulate loop heights, and different needle points are supplied to accommodate various weights of yarn.

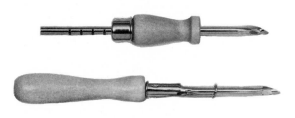

PUNCH NEEDLES

Estimating Amount of Material: Use the general rule that a 1-oz. skein of knitting worsted will cover approximately 6 sq. in. of backing; or one 70-yd. skein of cotton rug yarn will work approximately 8 sq. inches.

The foundation fabric is usually burlap or warp cloth, discussed in the section on hand hooking (page 1). The punch-needle designs are marked on the reverse side of rug fabric, as that is the side from which the needle is inserted. Directions for marking designs on fabric and for planning the finished edge (this must be done before hooking is begun) are on pages 165 and 162. The fabric is stretched taut on a rug frame (page 163), with the underside up.

HOOKING: Thread yarn through the needle eye in the point of the hook, following manufacturer's directions. Plunge needle through fabric and pull end of yarn through to reverse side. Always hold needle in vertical position. Next, lift needle slightly, bringing point just to top surface and over to position where next loop is to be placed. Plunge needle in as far as it goes to make each stitch. Continue making loops evenly spaced. At end of each skein or when changing colors, while point of needle is on reverse side, cut yarn halfway up needle. Push yarn end to reverse side and clip even with loops.

Be sure yarn feeds freely over the back of the hand and through the needle; otherwise uneven loops or none at all will result. While hooking succeeding rows, hold loops of finished row away from row being worked, with fingertips of left hand. This will keep the work even and loops from tangling.

In general, work motifs first, then background. Study pattern to decide which parts seem to be "on top" of adjoining parts (the shape that appears in front of the adjoining shapes), and work these parts first. Start by hooking outlines of motifs; do as much of one color as possible at one time. Then work background, first outlining each motif with a row of background color. Work background and design in straight rows, right to left, except the outlining. Some rugs with an allover pattern will be easier to work by starting at lower right corner with background color and working up to within one row of first motif. Then outline motif with one row of background color and one row of design color. Fill in motif and continue with background color.

When motifs and background have been completed within the frame, move fabric to a new working area, tacking finished portion to frame with thumbtacks or upholstery tacks to hold firmly.

If a row of loops is slightly lower than the surrounding rows, pull up with a knitting needle; pull up a single low loop with a crochet hook.

You may choose to contrast cut and uncut pile for an attractive effect. If so, complete the rug, then study the design and plan which areas you wish to trim to a velvety pile and which you wish to leave in the loop pile. Beveling may also be used to emphasize design areas or for shading.

Rug courtesy of American Thread Co.

ART DECO DIAMONDS RUG

Art Deco diamonds make a pretty border for a small rug, practical for bedside or bath, in acrylic yarn. Work it with a punch needle and skeins of yarn on a foundation fabric for a rug with a soft, looped pile.

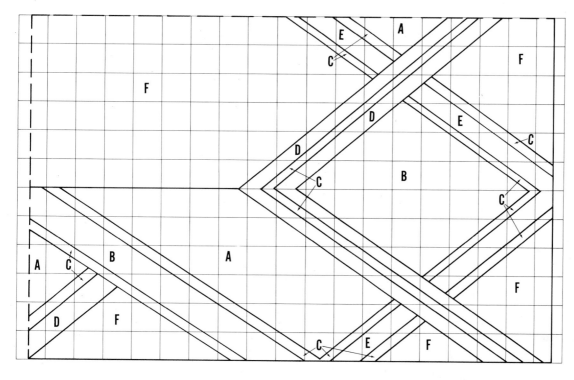

A LIGHT ORCHID
B CERISE
C HEMLOCK
D CHARTREUSE
E YELLOW
F NATURAL

SIZE: 23½" x 36".

EQUIPMENT: Punch needle. Sewing needle. Rectangular rug frame. Paper for pattern. Dressmaker's tracing (carbon) paper. Tracing paper. Yardstick. Scissors. Masking tape. Soft pencil. Thumbtacks or upholstery tacks. Glue (optional).

MATERIALS: Heavy rug yarn, 3-oz. skeins: light orchid, 2 skeins; cerise, 2 skeins; dark green, 2 skeins; chartreuse, 2 skeins; yellow, 1 skein; natural, 5 skeins. Foundation fabric (warp cloth, hopsacking, or burlap), 40" wide, ⅞ yd. Heavy-duty sewing thread.

DIRECTIONS: Preparing Foundation Fabric: Tape cut edges of foundation fabric to keep from raveling. On wrong side of fabric, mark outline of rug area, 23½" x 36", with yardstick and soft pencil, leaving equal margins all around. Mark lines through center of rug area in both directions, dividing marked rectangle into four equal sections. Enlarge quarter-pattern for rug by copying on paper ruled in 1" squares. Trace pattern. Place tracing over one of the quarter-sections, with border design along the outside; slip dressmaker's carbon between tracing and

foundation fabric and tape tracing in place. With a blunt point, such as the tip of a knitting needle, a dry ballpoint pen, or a soft pencil, go over lines of design to transfer to fabric. Repeat in each quarter section, reversing pattern to complete border design all around rug. To remove loose carbon, lay paper towels over design and press with hot iron. Go over lines with pencil to darken, if necessary.

To Hook Rug: Read general directions on page 21. Adjust needle to make loops ½" high. Practice making loops on scrap cloth before starting rug.

Work design first, following color key that accompanies pattern for yarn colors, then background. When rug design is complete, finish edges, following directions on page 162.

If desired, coat wrong side of rug with a mixture of half white (Sobo) glue and half water. Brush on glue, then let dry thoroughly.

Rug may also be lined. Cut lining same size as rug plus 1" all around. Turn under 1" margin; miter corners, trim, and slip-stitch. With carpet thread, slip-stitch lining to rug.

CHINESE RUG

Worked on cotton hopsacking, in rich, contrasting colors of rug yarn, this elegant Oriental motif blends with every decor.

SIZE: 36″ x 55″.

EQUIPMENT: Masking tape. Paper for pattern. Soft pencil. Ruler. Large piece of tracing paper. Dressmaker's tracing (carbon) paper. Rug frame. Scissors. Punch needle. Large, sturdy sewing needle.

MATERIALS: Warp cloth (100% cotton hopsacking), 52″ wide, 1¾ yds. Rug yarn: 30 60-yd. skeins rust; 21 skeins off-white. Heavy-duty sewing thread. Glue (optional).

DIRECTIONS: Tape cut edges of warp cloth to keep from raveling. Enlarge pattern by copying on paper ruled in 1″ squares. Complete design by repeating from *'s five times. Add the three rows of border pattern all around. Trace pattern. Center and tape pattern right side down on wrong side of warp cloth, with carbon paper between. With soft pencil, go over lines of design to transfer to warp cloth. Remove pattern and carbon. Go over lines with pencil to darken, if necessary. Design area is 36″ x 55″. The cloth stretches as it is worked, so rug will be a little larger when finished.

To Hook Rug: Read general directions on page 21. Following instructions that accompany the needle and referring to pattern, hook rug with punch needle. The shaded areas indicate rust color. Use rust color at needle setting #1; use off-white color at needle setting #5. Practice making loops on scrap cloth first before beginning to hook rug.

When design is complete, remove masking tape and trim margins to 3″ all around. Finish edges following directions on page 162.

If desired, coat wrong side of rug with a mixture of half white (Sobo) glue and half water. Brush on glue, then let dry thoroughly.

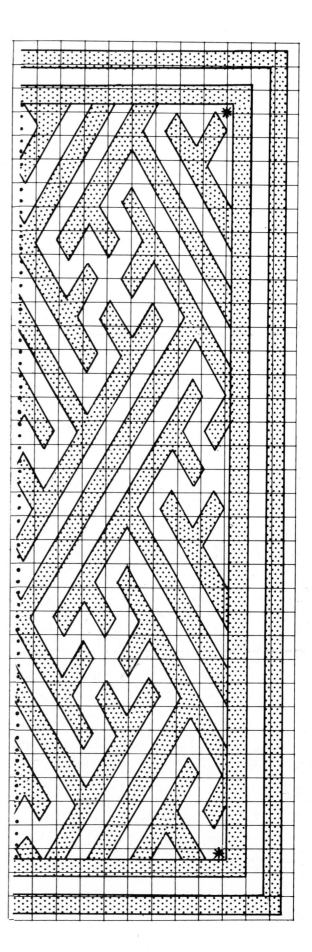

VENETIAN GRILLE RUG

This graceful motif, taken from a Venetian grille design, makes an elegant pattern for a punch-needle rug. The colors are dark taupe on a creamy background.

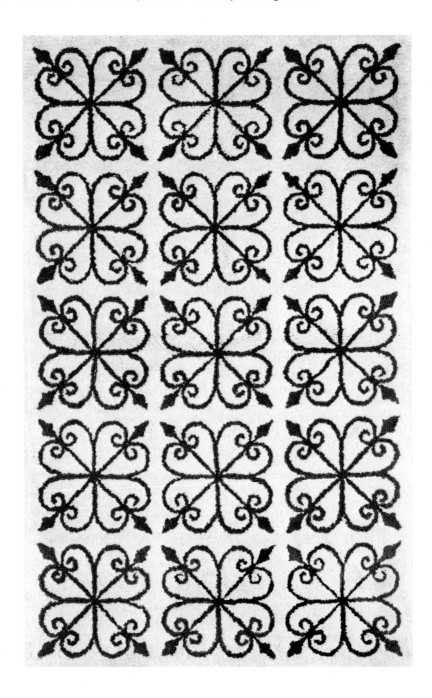

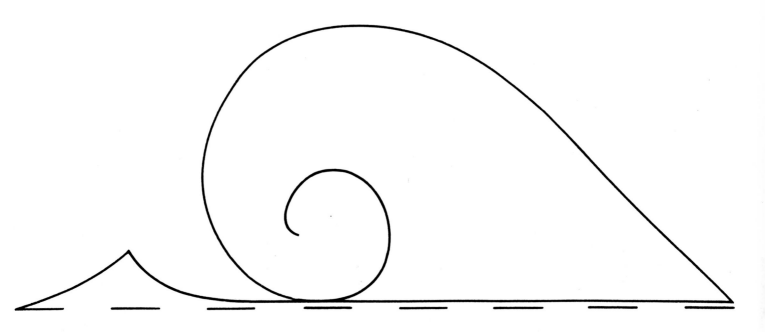

ACTUAL SIZE HALF-PATTERN FOR VENETIAN GRILLE RUG

SIZE: About 38″ x 62″.

EQUIPMENT: Punch needle. Large sewing needle. Rug frame. Tracing paper. Ruler. Soft pencil. Scissors. Dressmaker's tracing (carbon) paper. Blunt instrument (such as dry ballpoint pen) for transferring designs.

MATERIALS: Rug yarn, 120-yd. skeins: 38 natural, 10 dark taupe. Foundation fabric, 40″ wide, 2 yds. Rug binding, 5 yds. Carpet thread.

DIRECTIONS: Preparing Foundation Fabric: At center width of fabric (20″ from either selvage) draw a pencil line between two warp threads from top to bottom of fabric. It is not necessary to use yardstick; pencil will follow grain of cloth. Draw two more parallel lines from top to bottom, one on either side of center line, 12″ from center. Draw a line 1″ in from each selvage, for edge of rug.

At center of length of fabric (33″ from top and bottom) draw a line across fabric from selvage to selvage, at right angles to lines already drawn. Draw

four more parallel lines from selvage to selvage, two on either side of center line, spaced 12″ apart. Draw lines 5″ from top and bottom, for edge of rug.

Trace actual size half-pattern (indicated by dash lines) of complete quarter-motif shown above. Transfer pattern to fabric (see page 165), placing corner of pattern (center of complete motif) in right angle drawn in upper left corner; repeat three times around intersection of lines for one complete motif. Repeat around other intersections, making five rows of three motifs.

To Hook Rug: Read general directions on page 21. Starting with background color, work rug from lower right corner to first row of motifs. Work first motif, making all parts of design, except corners, two rows wide. Work background at right of motif, within motif, and up to next motif. Continue to end.

Remove rug from frame. Cut background loops, leaving loops of motifs uncut, if desired. Finish binding edges (directions on page 162).

MEXICAN BULLFIGHT RUG

This bold, dynamic design is based on an easy-to-follow symmetrical pattern to make a 48″ circular rug.

EQUIPMENT: Punch needle. Large sewing needle. Rug frame. Paper for patterns. Brown wrapping paper. Tracing paper. Straight pin. Fine wire. Ruler. Soft pencil. Glue. Scissors. Dressmaker's tracing (carbon) paper. Blunt instrument (such as dry ball-point pen) for transferring designs.

MATERIALS: Wool rug yarn in following colors and amounts: 1 oz. deep gold, ½ oz. wine, 3 oz. maroon, 5 oz. dark maroon, 4 oz. ivory, 8 oz. light taupe, 4 oz. medium taupe, 4 oz. dark taupe, 38 oz. light brown, 14 oz. medium brown, 19 oz. dark brown. Foundation fabric, 54″ square. Rug binding, 4¼ yds. Carpet thread.

DIRECTIONS: To Make Patterns: One-half of bull's-head motif is given on page 30, with the two small circles in correct position; enlarge by copying on paper ruled in 1″ squares. One-sixth of center motif and one-fourth of medallion are given actual size on page 31. Glue brown wrapping paper together to form a 54″ square. Using a pin, a pencil, and fine wire as a compass, draw a circle 4 ft. in diameter on brown paper. Divide circle into six equal parts and mark three center and three dash lines as shown on plan. Make a careful tracing of center motif, and transfer design to the brown-paper pattern, matching center lines, by going over lines on wrong side of tracing, then placing right side up on brown paper and going over lines again. Turn tracing around center point of motif, marking six complete sections of design. Make a tracing of half-pattern of bull's-head group. Mark on brown-paper pattern and flop tracing over the dividing line to complete. This is one-third of design around rug. Repeat tracing on center lines around rug (see plan). Trace quarter-pattern of medallion; flop tracing paper and trace again, to make complete half-pattern. Transfer to brown-paper pattern, matching dash lines (see plan); place outermost point of medallion about 2½″ from edge of rug. Repeat tracing around rug. Transfer pattern to foundation fabric, following directions on page 165.

To Hook Rug: Read general directions on page 21. Where lines of pattern are numbered, hook on line; numbered areas are to be filled in. Follow pattern and color key for placement of colors.

Remove completed design from frame and cut away excess foundation. Finish binding rug, following the directions on page 162.

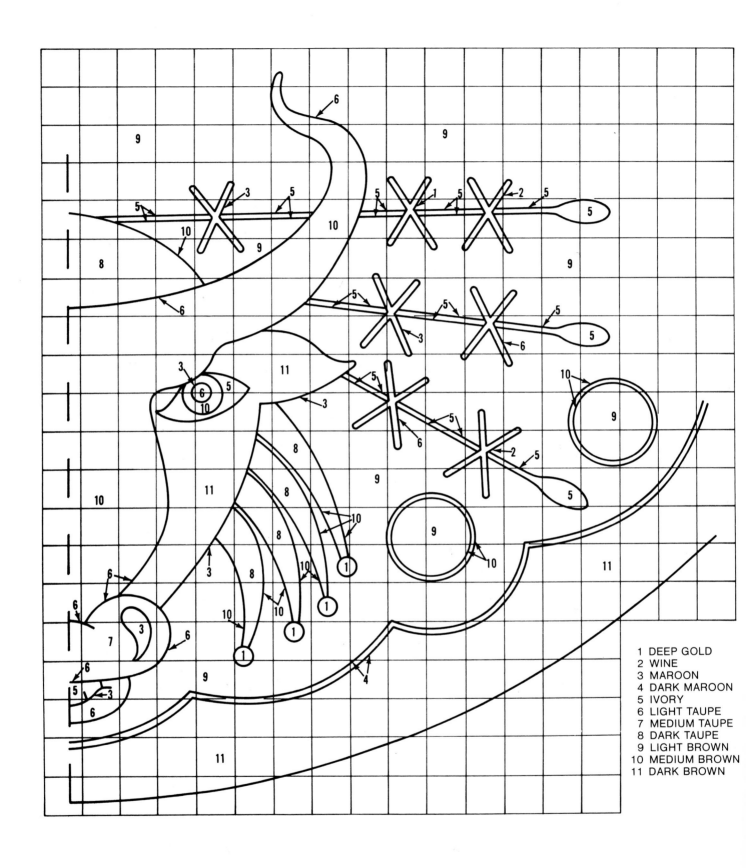

1 DEEP GOLD
2 WINE
3 MAROON
4 DARK MAROON
5 IVORY
6 LIGHT TAUPE
7 MEDIUM TAUPE
8 DARK TAUPE
9 LIGHT BROWN
10 MEDIUM BROWN
11 DARK BROWN

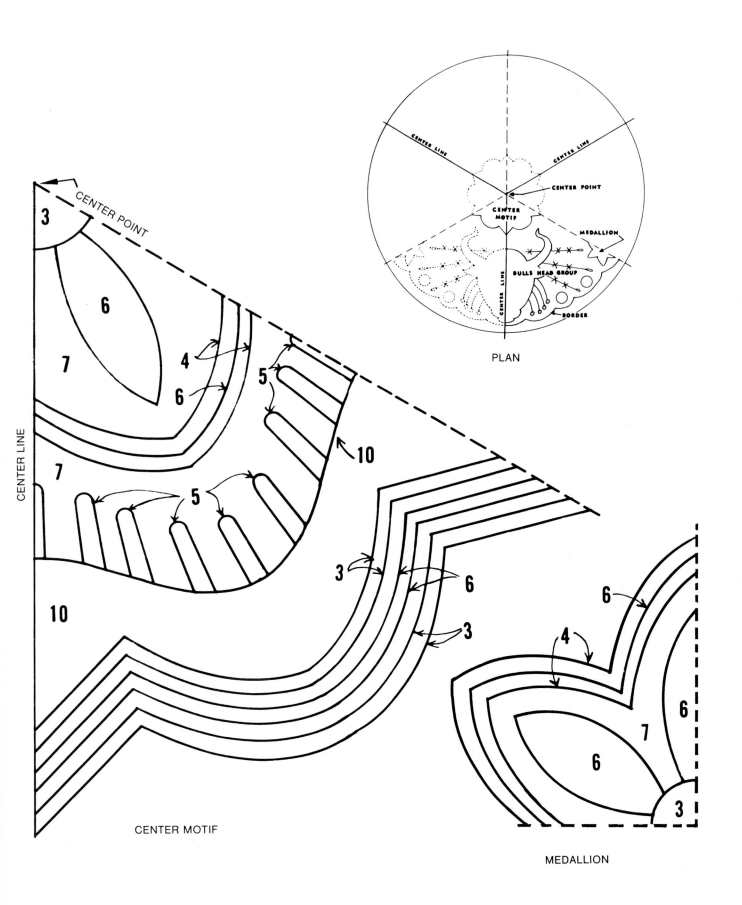

CENTER POINT

3

6

7

4

6

CENTER LINE

7

7

5

5

10

10

3

6

3

CENTER MOTIF

PLAN

CENTER LINE

CENTER LINE

CENTER POINT

CENTER MOTIF

MEDALLION

BULLS HEAD GROUP

BORDER

6

4

6

7

6

3

MEDALLION

GRACEFUL MALLARDS RUG

In muted shades of gray, white, and black, this charming scene from nature can be displayed as a wall panel, as shown, or used as an accent rug.

SIZE: 32" x 42".

EQUIPMENT: Punch needle. Large sewing needle. Rug frame. Paper for patterns. Tracing paper. Soft pencil. Carbon paper. Scissors. **For Framing:** Handsaw. Hammer. Stapler.

MATERIALS: Rug yarn, 1¾-oz. skeins: 15 white; 2 black; 2 light gray; 2 medium gray. Warp cloth, 40" x 50".

For Framing: Wood stripping, 1" wide, ¼" thick, 13 ft. Silver metallic, self-adhesive tape, 1¼" wide, 1 roll. Small finishing nails. Plywood, ¼" thick, 32" x 42". Masking tape.

For Rug: Carpet thread.

DIRECTIONS: Read general directions on page 21.

To Make Patterns: Enlarge patterns by copying on paper ruled in 1" squares. Find and mark center of warp cloth horizontally and vertically as a guide for placing ducks. Trace each section of duck panel patterns separately. Turn each tracing over so design will appear in reverse. Place single duck A to left of center vertical mark at bottom, allowing at least 4" margins at bottom and side. Place ducks B to right, matching the dotted lines to get correct placement. Transfer to cloth with carbon paper. Place single duck C at center, above others, as shown; place duck D to right at top; transfer as before. Mark outline of panel 32" x 42" with a 1" margin below water and grasses, and small equal margins at each side of farthest point of water.

To Hook Rug: Thread needle, following manufacturer's directions. Work loops about ¼" high. Make each punch about ¼" from last. Work ducks first, then grasses and water. Outline each section using color indicated by numbers on patterns (see color key). Fill in remainder of each area and work small details of design. When changing colors, push needle through cloth and cut yarn, leaving about 1" of yarn on underside (right side). Work background in white yarn; outline each design with two rows of white, then fill in rest of background to marked outline.

When hooking is finished, remove from frame and trim off all ends on front, making them even with loops.

For Rug: Trim away warp cloth margins to 2". Turn under ½" all around, then turn margin smoothly to back of rug and slip-stitch to back with carpet thread.

For Wall Panel: Stretch punchwork evenly and smoothly over ¼" plywood, 32" x 42". Turn all edges over to back and staple to plywood near edges of plywood. Trim all margins of cloth to 2" and tape edges to back of plywood.

Cut wood stripping to fit each side of panel, with butt joints. Cover each strip on one 1" surface and one edge, including ends, with a strip of silver tape. Place wood strips around plywood panel, silver side in and silver-covered edge extending ¼" on front beyond hooked loops; nail strip to edges of plywood. Cover outside 1" surface of wood strips with silver tape, overlapping tape on front edges.

NOTE: The drawings for the duck patterns have been perfected to give the ducks a more graceful shape than in the original hooked piece. Follow the patterns when doing the hooking. Inadvertently, as the hooking is done, the shapes broaden somewhat, which is the reason for the change in patterns.

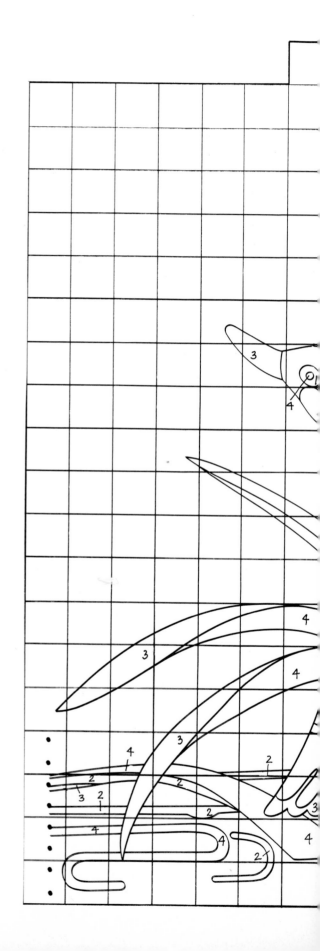

1 WHITE
2 LIGHT GRAY
3 MEDIUM GRAY
4 BLACK

DUCK A

35

DUCKS B

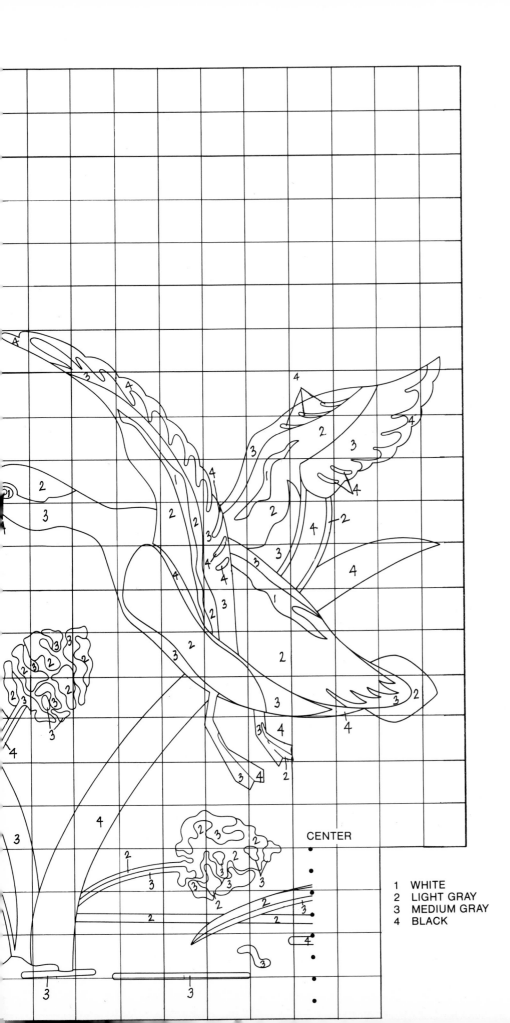

CENTER

1 WHITE
2 LIGHT GRAY
3 MEDIUM GRAY
4 BLACK

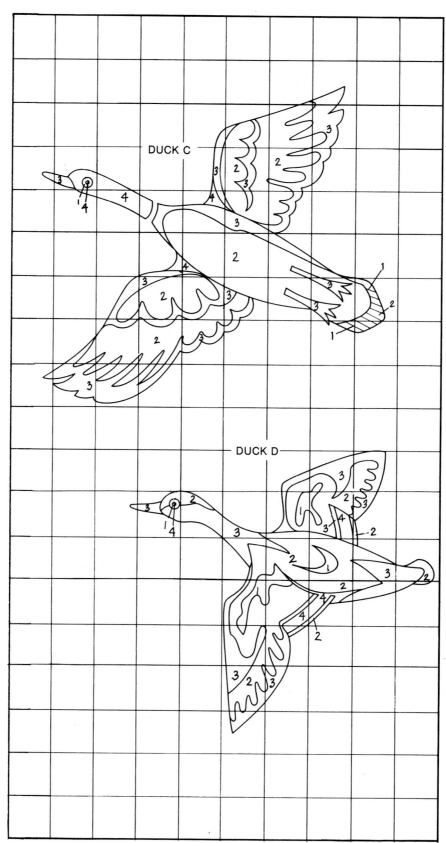

DUCK C

DUCK D

1 WHITE
2 LIGHT GRAY
3 MEDIUM GRAY
4 BLACK

3

Latch-Hooked Rugs

The knotted rug has an ancient history, beginning probably with nomadic tribes in Asia and developing to its highest form in Persia and Turkey around the sixteenth century. The rugs were made on looms, with the pile knotted in as the rug was woven—a technique also used in Scandinavia for the woven rya rugs.

Today we can achieve a deep-piled texture for rugs by knotting short strands of yarn on canvas with a latch (also called latchet) hook. This hook, developed in England about the mid-twenties, combines the hand hook with a latchet, taken from commercial knitting machines. It first became popular in the mid-thirties and continues to be a favorite.

general directions

MATERIALS AND EQUIPMENT: Wool rug yarn comes already cut into correct lengths for latch hooking, packaged according to color; or yarn from a skein may be cut into approximately 2½'' lengths by winding it around a piece of cardboard about 1¼'' deep and cutting with scissors. For ease in working, put each color into a separate plastic bag; mark each bag with the symbol for that color given in the chart's color key.

Canvas in a large mesh, usually 3⅓ or 4 meshes to the inch, is used with the latch hook.

No frame is used in latch hooking; the rug is worked in the lap or on a large table.

LATCH (LATCHET) HOOKING: Lay the canvas on a table, with the selvage edges at the sides and about 2'' of the canvas extending off the table toward you; roll up the other end of canvas. Before starting to work knots, turn four rows of the extended edge of canvas to front; work through this doubled canvas to form a finished end. If the width of the canvas equals the intended width of the rug, work across canvas from selvage to selvage. A large rug may be worked in sections and the sections sewn together (see Joining Canvas, page 163). If canvas is

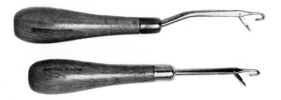

LATCH (LATCHET) HOOKS

wider than the rug, plan design from the center of canvas and work first row from center out to edges of design. Trim side edges of canvas to about 2'' (see Finishing, below).

Patterns for latch-hooked rugs may be bought with the designs painted on the canvas. The designs given in this book are in chart form; each square on chart represents one mesh on canvas.

The drawings (Figures 1-4) illustrate how to make knots with a latch hook. Fold yarn over shank of hook; hold ends with left hand (Fig. 1). With hook in right hand, hold latch down with index finger; push

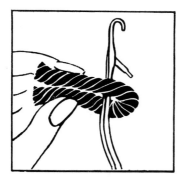

figure 1

figure 2

hook down through mesh of canvas, under double horizontal threads, and up through mesh above (Fig. 2). Draw hook toward you, placing yarn ends inside hook. Be sure yarn is completely inside the hook when the latch closes, so that end of hook does not snag or split the yarn (Fig. 3). Pull hook back through the canvas, drawing ends of yarn through loop; tighten knot by pulling ends with fingers (Fig. 4).

Yarn must be knotted on the weft threads—those running across the canvas from selvage to selvage. For an evenly knotted rug, work completely across canvas before starting next row. Work from right to left or left to right, whichever is more convenient.

Work rug to within five rows of the end. Cut off excess canvas beyond ten rows, turn up five rows, and work last five rows through doubled canvas, as at the beginning.

Finishing: Turn under side edges (leaving selvage edges on); slip-stitch firmly to back of rug with carpet thread. If there is excess canvas at the sides, fold to back of rug and baste in place. Sew rug binding to back over edges of canvas, stitching along both edges of binding with carpet thread.

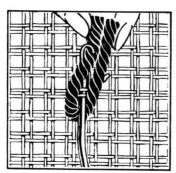

figure 3

figure 4

SCARLET TANAGER RUG

The scarlet tanager, framed in blossoms, is a delightful design taken from a hand-hooked rug of the Colonial era and reinterpreted here with a latch hook.

SIZE: 32" x 43".

EQUIPMENT: Latch (latchet) hook. Large-eyed needle. Scissors. Soft pencil.

MATERIALS: Packs of precut wool rug yarn: 24 tan; 6 hunter green; 5 coral; 4 black; 3 geranium red; 3 watermelon red; 3 turkey red; 2 jade green; 2 autumn brown. Rug canvas, 3⅓ mesh to the inch: 1 yd., 45" wide. Rug binding 4½ yds. Carpet thread.

DIRECTIONS: Read general directions on page 39. There are 134 squares across width of chart (long side); each square represents one knot stitch. Mark off 134 meshes in center of canvas by drawing a pencil line down each side. As rug is illustrated, there are five knots in background color all around rug which are not shown on chart. Follow chart on page 42 for design of rug, adding five rows of background color to beginning and end and five knots beyond each line at sides.

Finish sides according to directions on page 40.

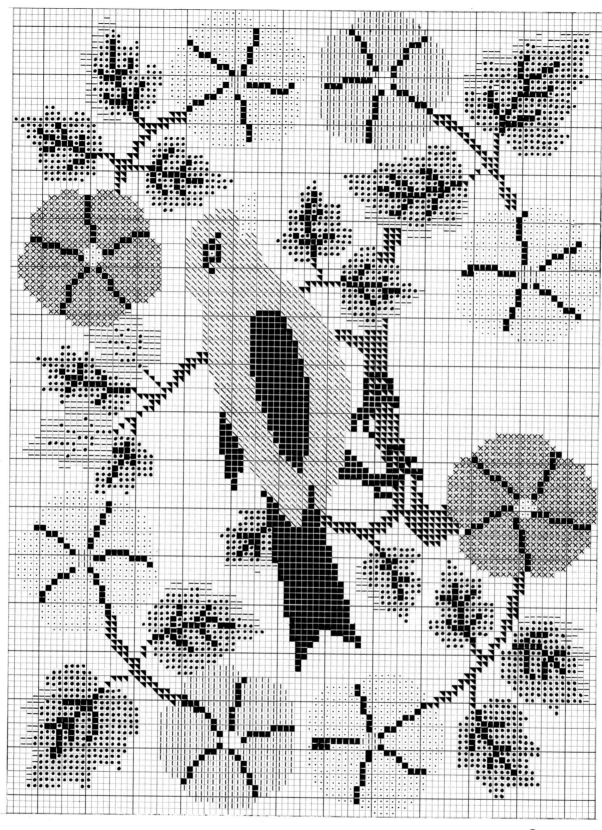

AUTUMN BROWN
BLACK
GERANIUM RED
TAN
CORAL
WATERMELON RED
JADE GREEN
HUNTER GREEN
TURKEY RED

PAISLEY RUG

A paisley pattern in a harmony of four reds makes a stunning accent for a traditional setting.

SIZE: 60" x 90".

EQUIPMENT: Latch (latchet) hook. Scissors. Large-eyed sewing needle.

MATERIALS: Precut wool rug yarn: geranium red, 20 packs; blue, 40½ packs; watermelon red, 25 packs; grass green, 13 packs; coral, 8 packs; dark red, 46½ packs. Rug canvas, 3⅓ mesh to the inch, 60" wide, 2¾ yds. Rug binding, 7 yds. Carpet thread.

DIRECTIONS: Read general directions on page 39. Place canvas on a flat surface, with selvages at sides. Rug is worked from half chart on pages 46 and 47, bottom to top. Each square of chart is a knot and each symbol on chart represents a different color (see color key). Leaving a 3" margin on canvas at bottom, knot first row of rug design in exact center of first row of meshes; be sure that there is an equal number of meshes on either side of first row (see Note below). Continue to work across in rows from right to left or left to right, as desired, until center of rug is reached. Turn chart around and work from center to far end. Do not turn rug while working, so that knots will always be made in the same direction.

When rug is finished, trim away canvas margin all around to about 1¼", tapering at center to edge of selvage. Turn margin to back of rug and sew securely in place with carpet thread. Finish according to directions on page 40.

Note: At center of rug, design will cover entire width of canvas, selvage to selvage. It is thus extremely important that rug be started and remain in exact center of canvas throughout knotting; chart must be followed carefully. An alternate method of working: Fold canvas in half widthwise and crease to mark center. Work first half of rug from center to end nearest you, following chart. Turn chart around and work second half from center to far end.

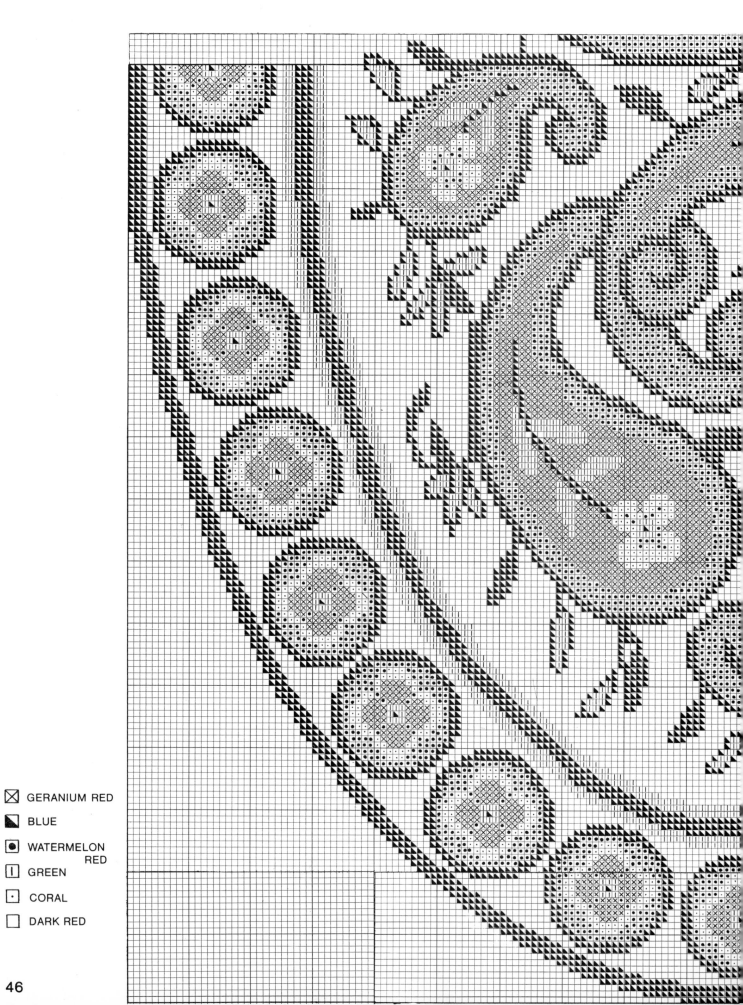

⊠ GERANIUM RED

◣ BLUE

⊙ WATERMELON
RED

Ⅰ GREEN

⊡ CORAL

☐ DARK RED

*do not repeat center row

VICTORIAN FRUITS RUG

A branch of abundant fruits makes a theme rich in nostalgia. Adapted from a Victorian rug that was hooked with fabric scraps, this project is worked with a latch hook and precut yarn.

SIZE: 30" x 50".

EQUIPMENT: Latch (latchet) hook. Scissors. Large-eyed sewing needle.

MATERIALS: Precut wool rug yarn: brown, 2 packs; medium green, 4 packs; watermelon red, 1½ packs; light green, 6½ packs; dark green, 5½ packs; tan, 31 packs; orange, 2 packs; purple, 2½ packs; golden brown, ½ pack. Rug canvas, 3⅓ mesh to the inch, 30" wide, 1½ yds. Rug binding, 4½ yds. Carpet thread.

DIRECTIONS: Read general directions on page 39. Place canvas on a flat surface with selvages at sides. To start, turn 1½" of canvas over to front, matching meshes, and work knots through the double canvas to make a finished edge. Starting at selvage, work across first row through double canvas, following first row at one end of chart on pages 50 and 51. Each square of chart is a knot; follow symbols in squares for colors. Background is worked in tan. Continue working rows across through double thickness. Work remainder of rug to opposite end through single canvas, up to last six rows of design on chart. Cut off canvas beyond twelve rows; turn over six rows to front and work last six rows through double canvas.

Finish according to directions on page 40.

■ DARK GREEN   ◧ MEDIUM GREEN   ⊟ LIGHT GREEN   ⊡ WATERMELON RED

☑ ORANGE   ◣ PURPLE   ■ BROWN   ☒ GOLDEN BROWN   ☐ TAN

ABC RUG

To add a whimsical touch to any child's room, the ABC motif is worked in rug yarn on 4-mesh-to-an-inch canvas with a latch hook; the background is cross-stitched.

SIZE: 32″ x 69″.

MATERIALS: Rug wool: beige, 42 skeins; light green, 17 skeins; dark green, 10 skeins; salmon, 14 skeins. Rug canvas, 4 meshes to the inch, 42″ wide, 2 yds. Rug-yarn cutter. Latch hook. Rug binding, 6 yds. Carpet thread. Large-eyed needle. Pencil. Ruler.

DIRECTIONS: Read general directions on page 39. Lay canvas out on a flat surface and mark outline of rug, 32″ x 69″. Following placement diagram, mark the top, bottom and sides of letters A and C and square for B on the canvas. Mark areas for single flowers and apples, spacing them as shown in illustration. The letters A and C and the square containing B are worked in latch-hook technique; the background, including apples and flowers, is worked in cross-stitch. Work rug sideways, across narrow width of canvas.

To do latch hooking, cut skeins of rug yarn into 3″ lengths, using rug-yarn cutter. Cut a good supply of each color before starting. Work the A first, then B square, then C, following charts.

When all latch-hook areas are complete, work the cross-stitch background (see cross-stitch details on this page). Be sure the top stitches and bottom stitches of all crosses are worked in same direction for an even appearance. Cut strands of yarn about 18″ long. To begin a strand, leave an end of yarn on back of canvas and work over this end. To end strand, run yarn back through a few stitches on wrong side and cut close to work. Work apples and flowers first, following charts on opposite page. Fill in the cross-stitch background to marked outline of rug and around letters, using beige yarn.

To finish, trim away unworked canvas, leaving 1½″ all around. Turn under this 1½″ margin of canvas and baste neatly in position on back of rug. Sew rug binding over unworked canvas on back.

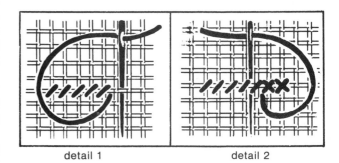

detail 1   detail 2

CROSS-STITCH

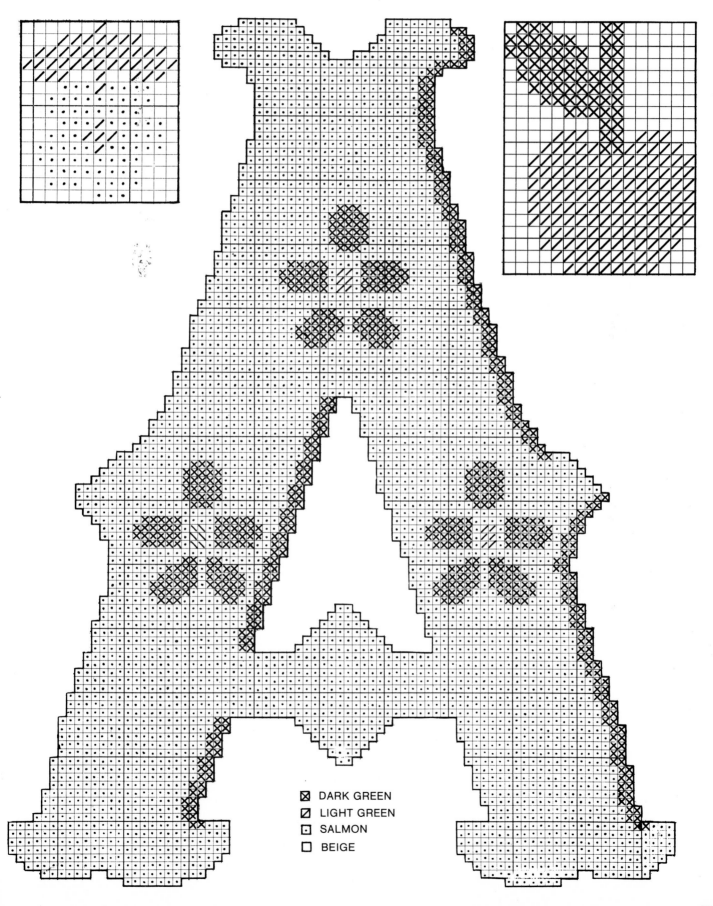

⊠ DARK GREEN
◩ LIGHT GREEN
⊡ SALMON
☐ BEIGE

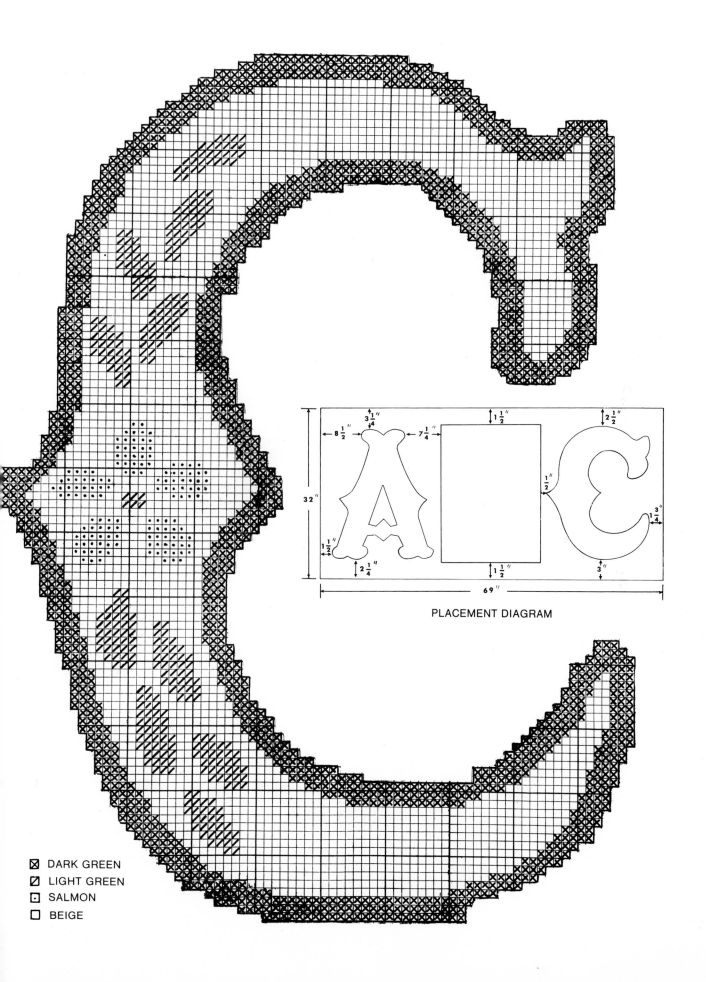

PLACEMENT DIAGRAM

⊠ DARK GREEN
⊿ LIGHT GREEN
⊡ SALMON
☐ BEIGE

BUTTERFLY RUG

A bold white butterfly is worked on a black background to create a vivid rug for decorating an entry, a bedside, or even a wall.

BLACK □
WHITE ☑

SIZE: 30″ x 50″

EQUIPMENT: Latch (latchet) hook. Scissors. Large-eyed sewing needle.

MATERIALS: Precut wool rug yarn: white, 18½ packs; black, 35 packs. Rug canvas, 3⅓ mesh to the inch, 30″ wide, 1½ yds. Rug binding, 4½ yds. Carpet thread.

DIRECTIONS: Read general directions on page 39. Place canvas on a flat surface, with selvages at sides. To start, turn 1″ of canvas over to front, matching meshes, and work knots through the double canvas to make a finished edge. Starting at selvage, work across first row through double canvas, following bottom row of chart. Each square of chart is a knot; filled-in squares are worked in white and blank squares are worked in black. Continue working through the double canvas. Work remainder of rug to opposite end through single canvas, up to the last five rows of design on chart. Cut off canvas beyond ten rows; turn five rows of canvas over to front and work last five rows through double canvas.

Finish according to directions on page 40.

SAROUK RUG AND FLOOR CUSHION

Latch hook an Oriental garden. Rich, deep rust makes a luxuriant background for this Oriental pair. The rug has exotic blossoms, a handsome border; the cushion repeats the central motif with some adaptations.

RUG SIZE: 36″ x 72″.
CUSHION SIZE: 26″ square.
EQUIPMENT: Latch (latchet) hook. Scissors. Rug needle for binding. Strong sewing needle for cushion.
MATERIALS: Rug: Rug canvas, 3⅓ mesh per inch, 36″ wide, 2⅙ yds. Precut turkey rug wool: 3 packs royal blue; 4 packs each of cream, orange-red, old gold; 8 packs leaf green; 10 packs dark green; 18 packs tan; 43 packs dark rust. 100-gram skein of dark rust wool for binding. **Floor Cushion:** Rug canvas, 27″ wide, 1 yd. Precut turkey rug wool: 1 pack each of cream, orange-red, royal blue, old gold; 2 packs each of leaf green and tan; 3 packs dark green; 18 packs dark rust. Rust-colored corduroy fabric, 1 yd. About 4 to 5 lbs. cotton or dacron for stuffing. Rust-colored heavy-duty sewing thread.

DIRECTIONS: Rug: Rug design is 119 squares wide and 239 squares long. Mark the center of your canvas, then mark the area of rug design on canvas.

Read general directions on page 39. Work the first row of knots through doubled canvas from center to left edge. When rug is finished the last squares of canvas on each selvage edge will be covered with binding stitch. Hook rug, following the chart. Chart is for one-quarter of the design. Each square on chart represents one square on canvas. Continue to work across in rows from right to left or left to right, as

desired, until one-quarter is completed. Repeat chart in reverse, omitting center row, to finish one half. Continue to work second half above, reversing chart, and again omitting center row, until you get to within the last four rows of design. Fold canvas under and work last four rows through doubled canvas, as you did at the start. Trim off excess canvas on wrong side.

To bind edges, follow details and instructions below, using the dark rust skein yarn.

CUSHION: Cushion is 89 squares wide and long. Mark design area in center of canvas; mark center. Do not turn canvas under. Use only the center of design for cushion. Bottom edge starts at row marked by an X on chart; the side edge ends ten rows beyond starred row. Refer to illustration; omit the dark green leaf and tan leaf at each side of center; work only the inner portion of lower flower on each side consisting of tan, dark rust, orange-red, and old gold. Fill in these areas with dark rust background color. When finished, trim canvas edges to 1″.

To finish pillow, cut corduroy the same size as canvas. With right sides facing, sew edges together, making 1″ seams; leave a large opening in center of one side. Trim seams. Turn to right side. Stuff pillow fully. Turn edges of opening in and slip-stitch closed.

TO BIND EDGES

Turn rug over with bottom side up. Thread needle and start with a few close overcast stitches to secure. Insert the needle in first hole, pull out toward you. Make next stitch in fourth hole; then back to second, forward to fifth, back to third, forward to sixth, etc.

Rug courtesy of Woolcraft, Inc.

☐ DARK RUST ▨ TAN ◪ DARK GREEN ⊡ LEAF GREEN ⊠ OLD GOLD ⊟ ORANGE-RED

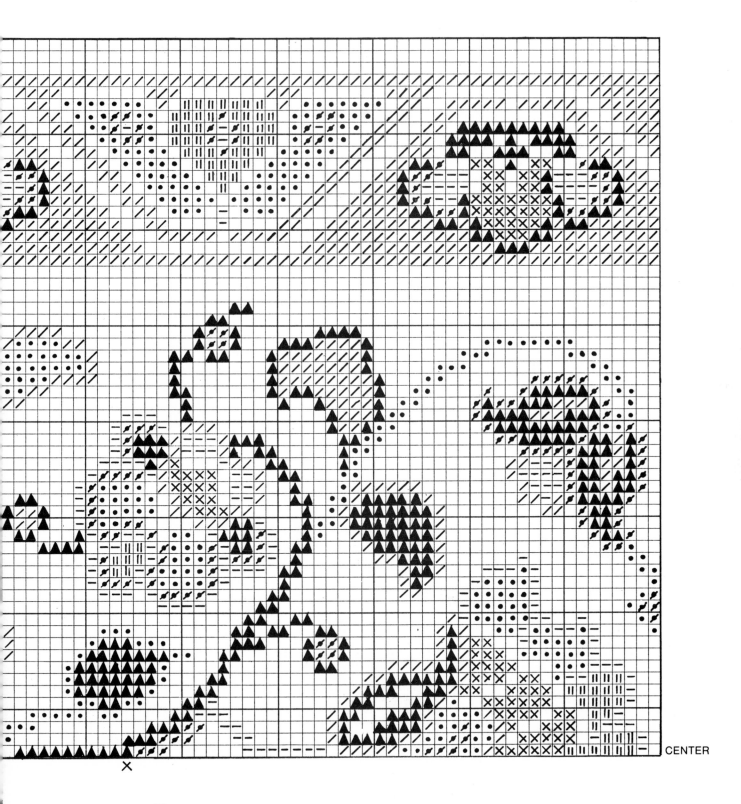

CENTER

◩ CREAM   ⦀ ROYAL BLUE

DIAMOND-STRIPED RUNNER

Vibrant, sunny colors make a foyer truly welcoming! The runner is patterned in diamonds and stripes and measures 30″ wide; it can be made to any convenient length.

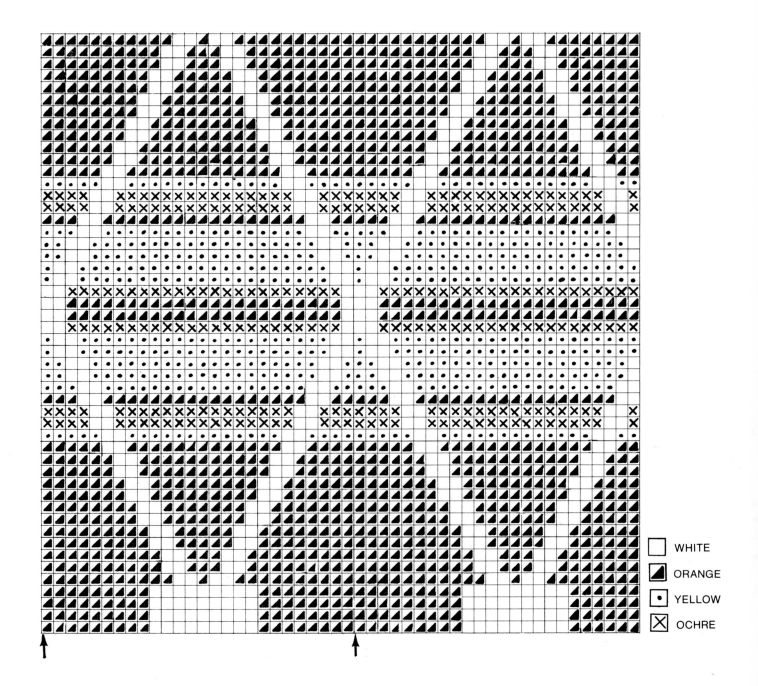

☐	WHITE
◣	ORANGE
⊡	YELLOW
☒	OCHRE

EQUIPMENT: Latch (latchet) hook. Large-eyed needle. Scissors.

MATERIALS: Packs of precut wool rug yarn (amounts are given for one diamond stripe repeated across width of rug as per chart): 8¼ orange, 3¼ yellow, 2¾ white, 1¾ ochre. Rug canvas, 3⅓ mesh to the inch, 30″ wide; length of runner plus 5″ (see below). Rug binding, twice length of runner. Carpet thread.

DIRECTIONS: Read general directions on page 39. Chart gives complete diamond-stripe pattern, which works out to be 15″ deep on canvas. This

stripe can be repeated to make length of runner desired. To figure length of canvas, multiply desired number of lengthwise diamond stripes by 15 and add 5″, for total length of canvas.

Starting at lower right corner of chart, work across canvas to left, from selvage to selvage, repeating portion between arrows; omit last three rows at left side of chart to finish left-hand edge of runner the same as right edge. At end of runner, work first four rows of chart to make both ends the same.

Finish side edges with rug binding according to directions on page 40.

PLAID RUG

Textured plaid is created with vertical stripes of regular rug wool crossed by horizontal stripes of longer rya yarn. A perfect hall runner.

RUST ☒
GREEN ▯
RED ◹
ROSE ⊡

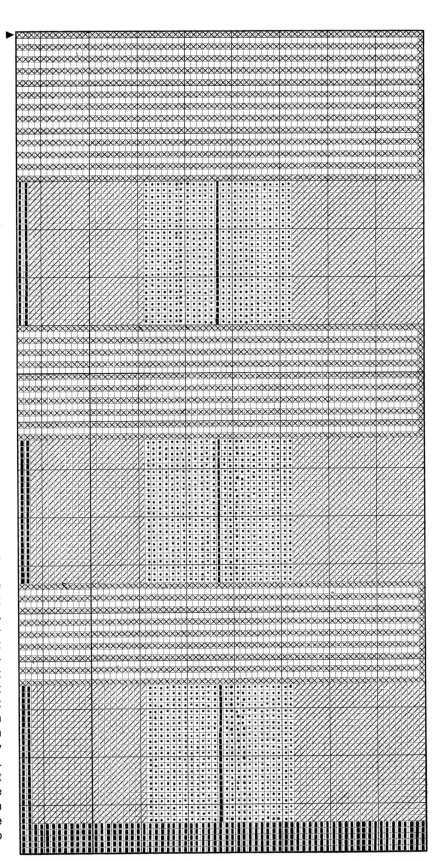

SIZE: 36″ x 72″.

EQUIPMENT: Latch (latchet) hook. Scissors. Large-eyed sewing needle.

MATERIALS: Precut rug yarn, 1-oz. unit packs: red, 36 packs; rose, 21 packs; green, 6 packs. Precut rya rug yarn, 1½-oz. units packs, 3 strand: rust, 47 packs. Rug canvas, 4 mesh to the inch, 36″ wide, 2¼ yds. Rug binding, 6 yds. Carpet thread.

DIRECTIONS: Read general directions on page 39. Place canvas on a flat surface, with selvages at sides. To start, turn five rows of canvas over to front, matching meshes, and work knots through the double canvas to make a finished edge. Starting at selvage, work across first row through double canvas, right to left, following bottom row of chart. Chart is for one-quarter of pattern. Arrows at top of chart indicate center rows. When working across, repeat design in reverse for second half of each row. Each square of chart represents a knot. The rows of X's on chart are worked with rya yarn (3 strands), and every other row is left unworked (blank rows on chart). Continue working rug to top of chart; then repeat bottom half in reverse until you get to within five rows of end. Cut off canvas beyond ten rows; turn five rows of canvas over to front and work last five rows through double canvas. Finish according to directions on page 40.

THREE "PATCHWORK" RUGS

Traditional patchwork quilt motifs inspired these three modern rugs, worked with the latch hook. Log Cabin, Swing-in-the-Center, and Contemporary Patchwork are all repeat designs that adapt easily to larger size rugs.

LOG CABIN

CONTEMPORARY PATCHWORK

SWING-IN-THE-CENTER

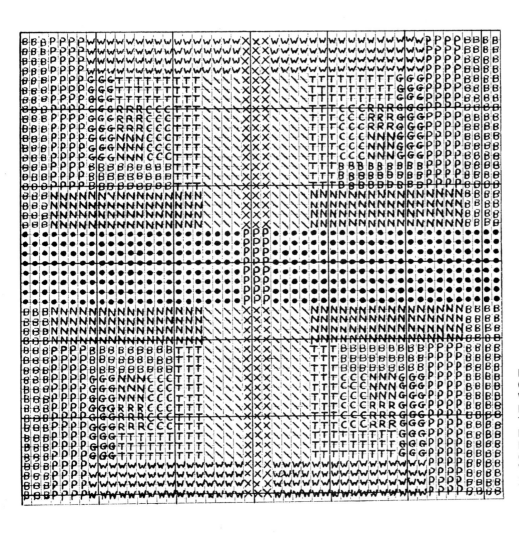

P ROYAL BLUE
G SPRUCE GREEN
W WHITE
B HYDRANGEA BLUE
T SOFT TURQUOISE
R TURKEY RED
N BRIGHT NAVY
C SPRING GREEN
\ LIGHT GRAY
X DARK GRAY
● BLACK

log cabin rug

SIZE: 30″ x 43″.

EQUIPMENT: Latch (latchet) hook. Scissors. Large-eyed needle.

MATERIALS: Packs of precut wool rug yarn: 9 hydrangea blue; 6 royal blue; 3 spruce green; 6 bright navy; 6 soft turquoise; 3 spring green; 3 turkey red; 6 white; 9 black; 6 light gray; 3 dark gray. Rug canvas, 3⅓ mesh to the inch, 30″ wide, 47″ long. Rug binding, 2½ yds. Carpet thread.

DIRECTIONS: Read general directions on page 39. Follow chart for repeat design of rug. Each square of chart represents one knot. Design is repeated six times for rug illustrated—twice across width, three times for length. For longer rug, extend length of canvas 15″ for each repeat section.

Finish sides of rug; see page 40.

O TURKEY RED
● BLACK
\ WHITE
X GRASS GREEN

swing-in-the-center
rug

SIZE: 30″ x 43″.
EQUIPMENT: Latch (latchet) hook. Scissors. Large-eyed needle.
MATERIALS: Packs of precut wool rug yarn: 6 turkey red; 18 grass green; 18 white; 9 black. Rug canvas, 3⅓ mesh to the inch, 30″ wide, 47″ long. Rug binding, 2½ yds. Carpet thread.
DIRECTIONS: See directions for Log Cabin Rug.

V	DARK GRAY
\	LIGHT GRAY
●	BLACK
O	WHITE
X	TURQUOISE

contemporary patchwork rug

SIZE: 27″ x 48″.

EQUIPMENT: Latch (latchet) hook. Scissors. Large-eyed needle.

MATERIALS: Packs of precut wool rug yarn: 8 black; 16 turquoise; 12 dark gray; 8 light gray; 12 white. Rug canvas, 3⅓ mesh to the inch, 30″ wide, 52″ long. Rug binding, 54″. Carpet thread.

DIRECTIONS: Read general directions on page 39. Follow chart for repeat design of rug. Each square of chart represents one knot. Design is repeated eight times for rug illustrated—twice across width, four times for length. For longer rug extend length of canvas 13½″ for each repeat section.

Finish sides of rug; see page 40.

LIGHTNING RUNNER

A slash of color to make any width, any length—just continue the pattern until you reach the size you need.

SIZE: 19½" x 59".

EQUIPMENT: Latch (latchet) hook. Scissors. Large-eyed sewing needle. Pencil. Ruler. Cardboard.

MATERIALS: Heavy rug yarn, 70-yd. skeins: red, 11 skeins; orange, 5 skeins; watermelon pink, 4 skeins; natural or white, 3 skeins. Rug canvas, 4 mesh to the inch, 32" wide, 1¾ yds. Rug binding, 4½ yds. Carpet thread.

DIRECTIONS: Read general directions on page 39. With pencil, mark off area of canvas to be worked, 19½" x 59", leaving at least 2" margins all around. Trim off excess canvas.

Cut rug yarn into 3" lengths by winding it around a strip of cardboard 1½" wide and cutting yarn with scissors along one edge of cardboard. **Note:** To insure uniform lengths of yarn, do not wrap more than three layers around cardboard.

Place canvas on a flat surface with selvages at sides. To start, turn five rows of canvas over to front, matching meshes, and work knots through the double canvas to make finished edge. Work across first row through double canvas, following bottom row of chart. Each square of chart is a knot; follow symbols for colors. Continue working rows across through double thickness. Work remainder of rug to opposite end through single canvas, up to last five rows of design on chart. Cut off canvas beyond ten rows; turn over five rows to front and work last five rows through double canvas.

Finish according to directions on page 40.

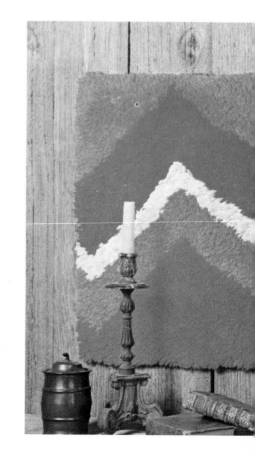

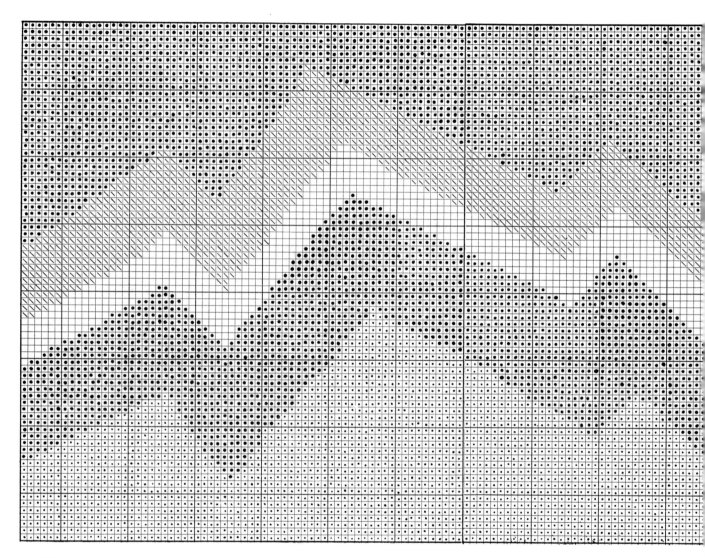

⊡ RED
⊡ ORANGE
◨ PINK
☐ WHITE

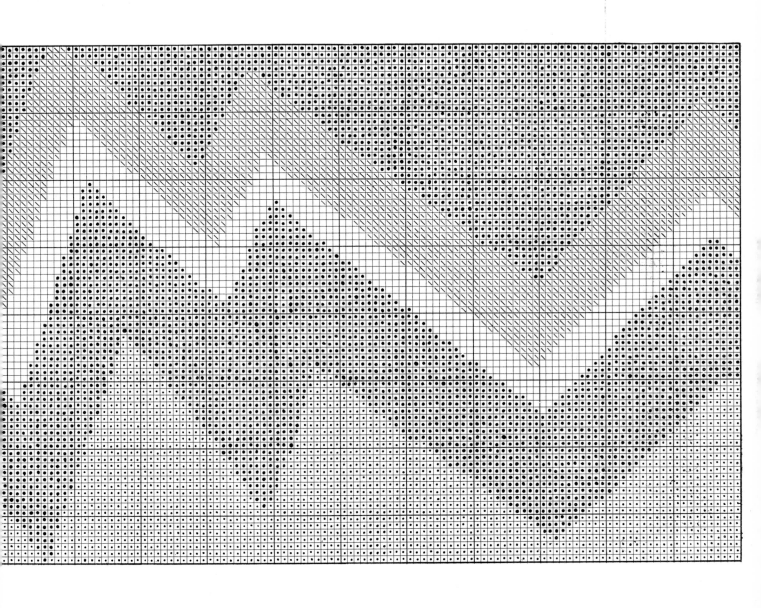

LEAF SHADOW RUG

Slender branches cast their deep green shadows on a ground of paler green. The rug is worked on 4-mesh-to-the-inch canvas.

SIZE: 32″ x 56″.

EQUIPMENT: Latch (latchet) hook. Scissors. Large-eyed sewing needle.

MATERIALS: Precut rug wool, 1-oz. unit packs: dark green, 16 packs; light green, 53 packs. Rug canvas, 4 mesh to the inch, 32″ wide, 1⅔ yds. Rug binding, 3¼ yds. Carpet thread.

DIRECTIONS: Read general directions on page 39. Place canvas on a flat surface, with selvages at sides. To start, turn 1½″ of canvas over to front, matching meshes, and work knots through the double canvas to make a finished edge. Starting at selvage, work across first row through double canvas, following first row at one end of chart on pages 76 and 77. Each square of chart is a knot; blank squares are light green, filled-in squares are dark green. Continue working five more rows across through double thickness. Work remainder of rug to opposite end through single canvas, up to last six rows of design on chart. Cut off canvas beyond twelve rows; turn over six rows to front, and work last six rows through double canvas.

Finish according to directions on page 40.

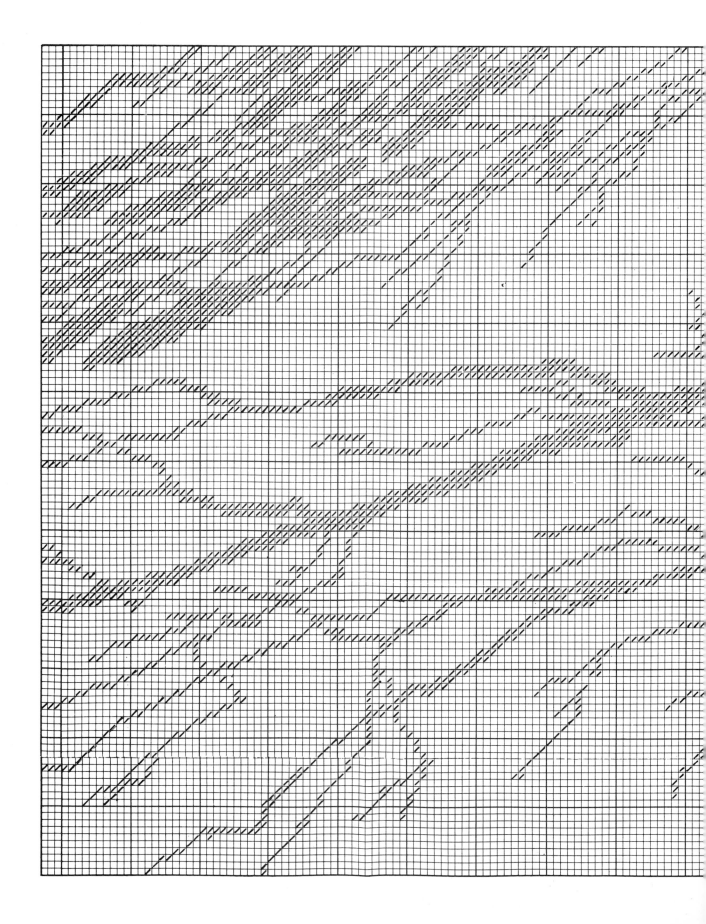

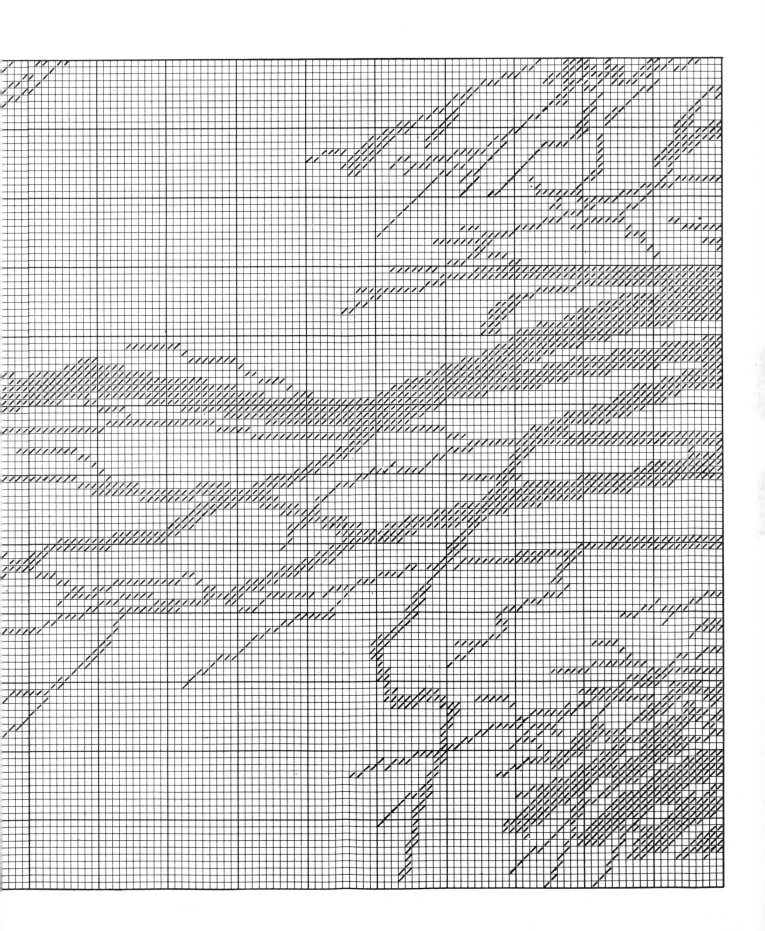

GARDEN PATHWAYS RUG

A gentle pattern flows in muted colors to complement a harmonious environment.

SIZE: 40″ x 58″.

EQUIPMENT: Latch (latchet) hook. Scissors. Large-eyed sewing needle.

MATERIALS: Precut rug wool, 1-oz. unit packs: lime, 28 packs; light olive, 30 packs; rose, 18 packs; cream, 18 packs. Rug canvas, 4 mesh to the inch, 42″ wide, 1¾ yds. Rug binding, 4 yds. Carpet thread.

DIRECTIONS: Read general directions on page 39. Place canvas on a flat surface, with selvages at sides. To start, turn 1″ of canvas over to front, match meshes, and work latch-hook knots through double canvas for four rows, to make a finished edge. Starting 1″ in from right-hand side, work first row across, following chart color key to work the pattern. Continue across row to left side, following chart. Work remainder of rug to opposite end through single canvas, up to last four rows of design on chart. Cut off canvas beyond eight rows; turn four rows of canvas over to front and work last four rows through double canvas.

Finish according to directions on page 40.

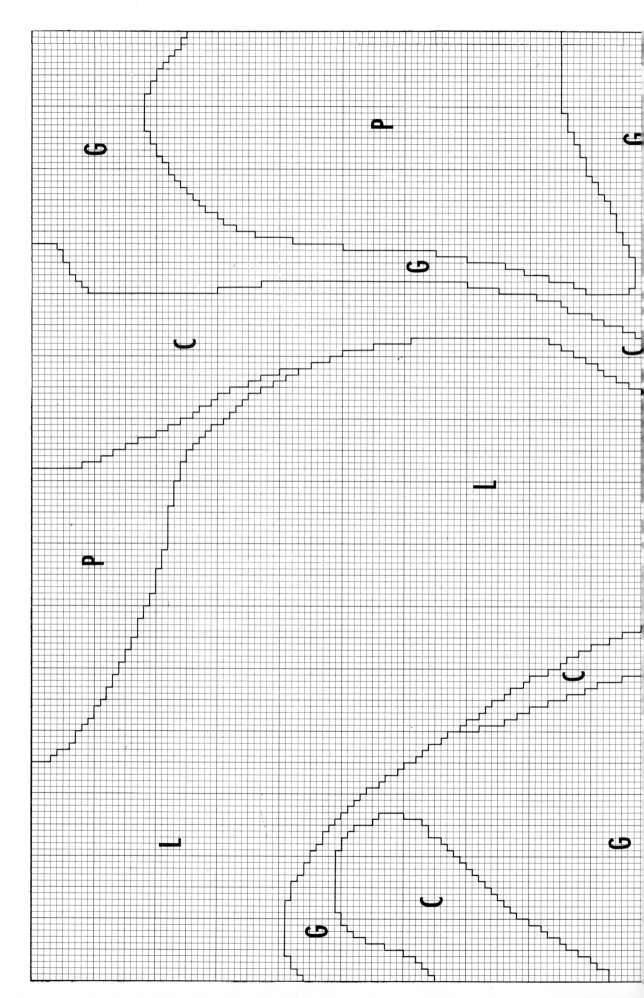

G LIGHT OLIVE
L LIME
P ROSE
C CREAM

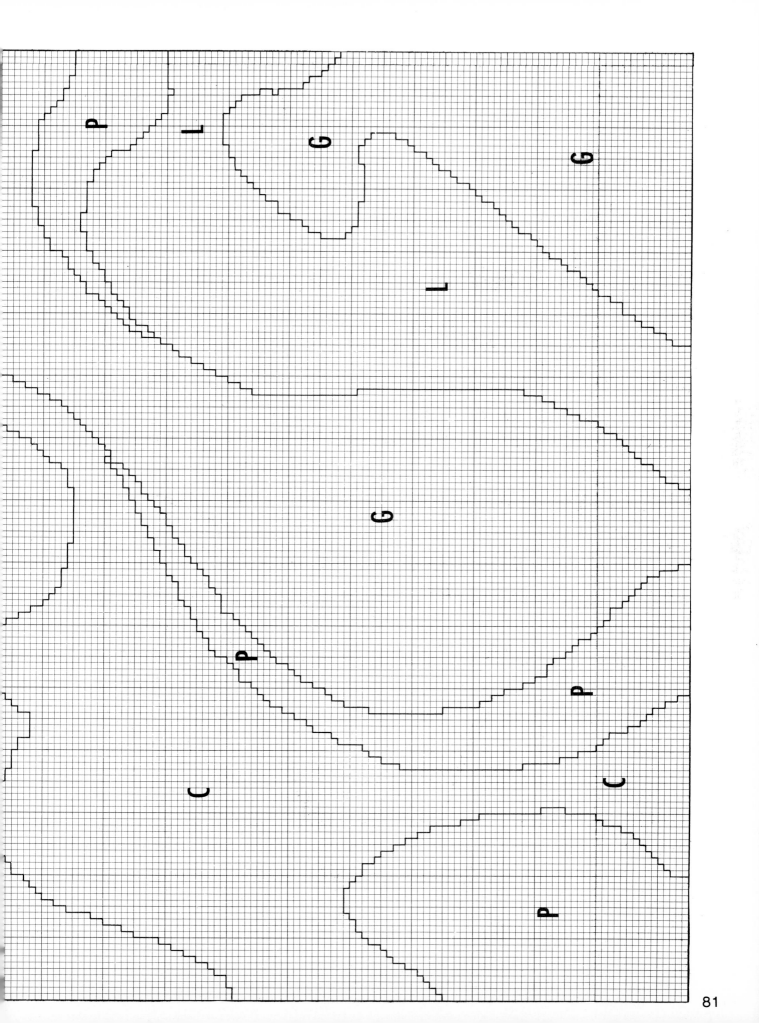

TROPICAL GARDEN RUG

Here is a garden of tropical flowers to hook in exotic colors on 4-mesh-to-the-inch canvas, using precut rug wool.

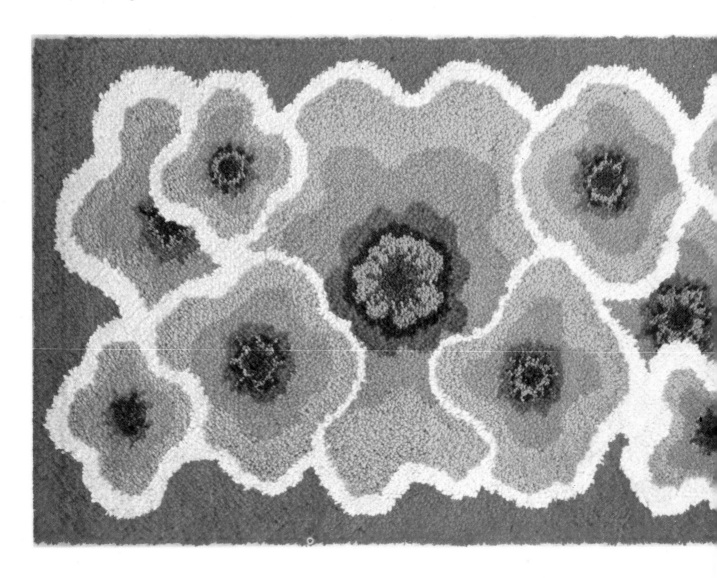

SIZE: 30″ x 48½″.

EQUIPMENT: Latch (latchet) hook. Scissors. Large-eyed sewing needle. Pencil. Ruler.

MATERIALS: Precut rug yarn, 1-oz. unit packs: white, 18 packs; pink, 16 packs; orange. 10 packs; gold, 13 packs; violet, 3 packs; chartreuse, 2 packs; dark rose, 2 packs; dark green, 1 pack. Rug canvas, 4 mesh to the inch, 36″ wide, 1½ yds. Rug binding, 3 yds. Carpet thread.

DIRECTIONS: Read general directions on page 39. With pencil mark off area of canvas to be worked, 30″ wide, leaving equal margins at sides.

Place canvas on a flat surface, with selvages at sides. To start, turn 1″ of canvas over to front, matching meshes, and work knots through the double canvas to make a finished edge. Work first row through double canvas, following bottom row of chart on pages 84 and 85. Each square of chart is a knot; each symbol on chart is a different color (see color key). Continue working through the double canvas; work remainder of rug to opposite end through single canvas, up to last six rows of design on chart. Cut off canvas beyond twelve rows; turn six rows of canvas over to front and work last six rows through double canvas.

Finish according to directions on page 40.

WHITE

GOLD

PINK

ORANGE

VIOLET

DARK ROSE

CHARTREUSE

DARK GREEN

"GLOWING EMBERS" RUG

A swirl of warm colors—orange, pink, cinnamon, and copper—suggests reflected firelight! A perfect hearthside rug—or hang it on a wall opposite the fire.

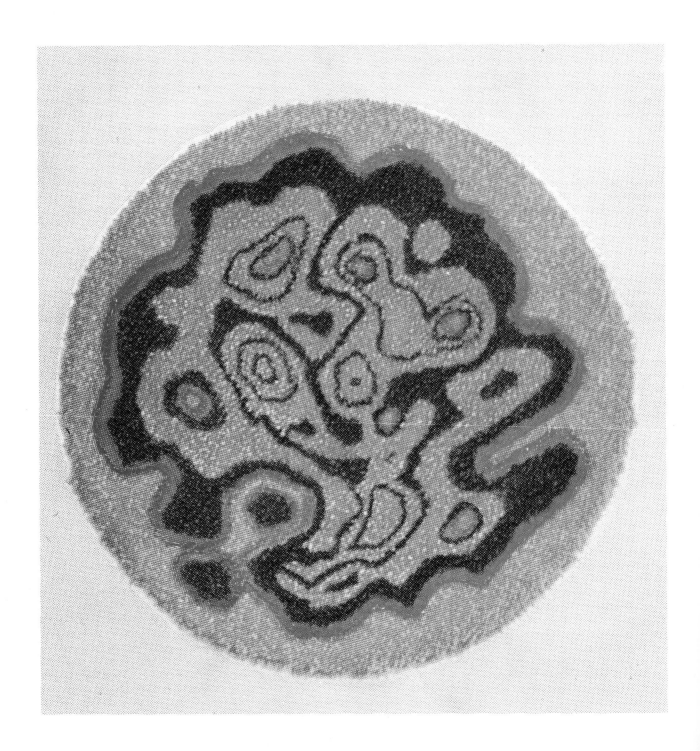

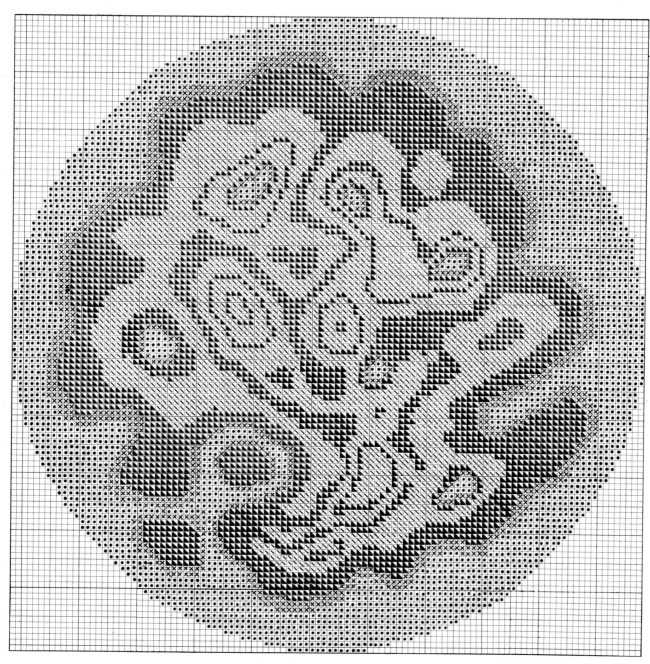

☐ ORANGE   ☒ PINK   ◪ CINNAMON   ◩ ROSE

SIZE: 30″ diameter.

EQUIPMENT: Latch (latchet) hook. Scissors. Large-eyed sewing needle.

MATERIALS: Precut rug yarn, 1-oz. unit packs: pink, 3 packs; cinnamon, 9 packs; rose, 8 packs; orange, 9 packs. Rug canvas, 4 mesh to the inch, 36″ square. Rug binding, 2¾ yds. Carpet thread.

DIRECTIONS: Read general directions on page 39. Place canvas on a flat surface, with selvages at sides. Leaving a 3″ margin of canvas, start rug at bottom, working across in rows from right to left or left to right, whichever seems more convenient. Following chart, work first row of latched knots across center area. Each square of chart is a knot. Continue working from chart to make round rug design.

When rug is finished, trim away canvas margin all around to about 1¼″. Turn this margin to back of rug and sew securely in place with carpet thread. Finish according to directions on page 40.

SUNRISE RUG

A textured rug that suggests the radiance of the southwestern sky at sunrise. Regular rug wool makes the sunray part of the design; the cloudlike center is worked with a longer, three-strand rya yarn to form high-pile relief.

SIZE: 37″ x 57″.

EQUIPMENT: Latch (latchet) hook. Scissors. Large-eyed sewing needle.

MATERIALS: Precut rug yarn, 1-oz. unit packs: white, 14 packs; yellow, 20 packs; light yellow, 23 packs; light brown, 8 packs; gold, 2 packs; brick, 2 packs. Precut rya rug yarn, 1½-oz. unit packs, 3 strand: white smoke, 22 packs. Rug canvas, 4 mesh to the inch, 37″ wide, 1¾ yds. Rug binding, 3¼ yds. Carpet thread.

DIRECTIONS: Read general directions on page 39. Place canvas on a flat surface, with selvages at sides. To start, turn 1½″ of canvas over to front, matching meshes, and work knots through the double canvas to make a finished edge. Starting at selvage, work across first row through double canvas, following bottom row of chart on pages 90 and 91. Each square of chart is a knot, except for blank squares; blank squares on chart (in rya-yarn section only) are left unworked. Continue working five more rows across through the double canvas; work remainder of rug to opposite end through single canvas, up to last six rows of design on chart. Cut off canvas beyond twelve rows; turn six rows of canvas over to front and work last six rows through double canvas.

Finish according to directions on page 40.

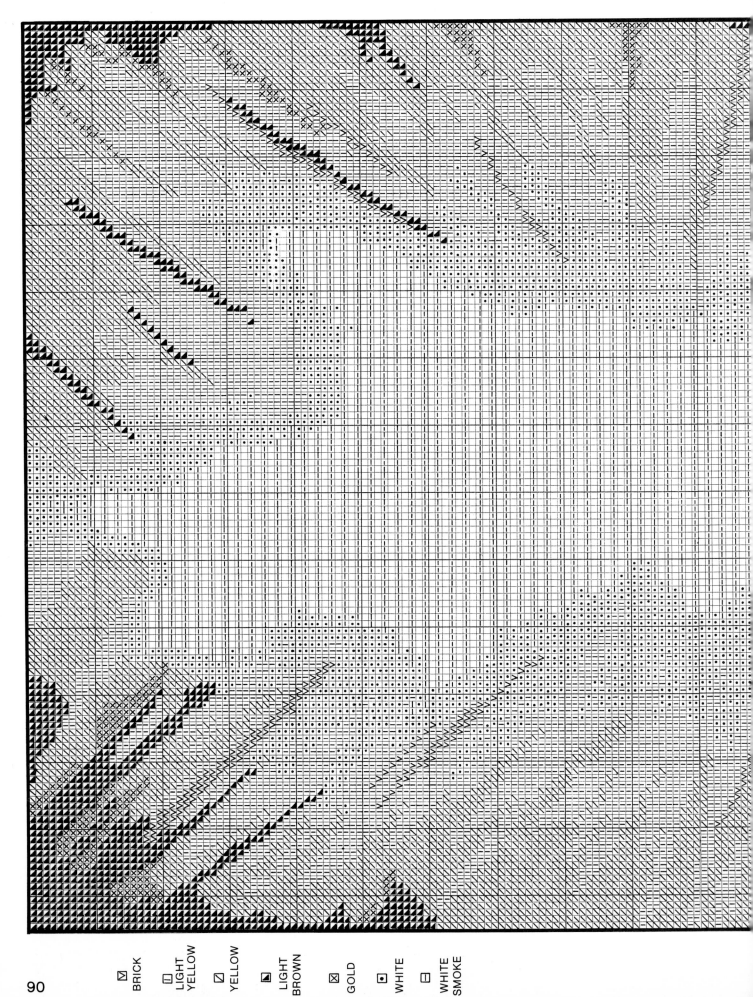

90

⊠ BRICK

☐ LIGHT YELLOW

☑ YELLOW

◣ LIGHT BROWN

⊠ GOLD

⊡ WHITE

⊟ WHITE SMOKE

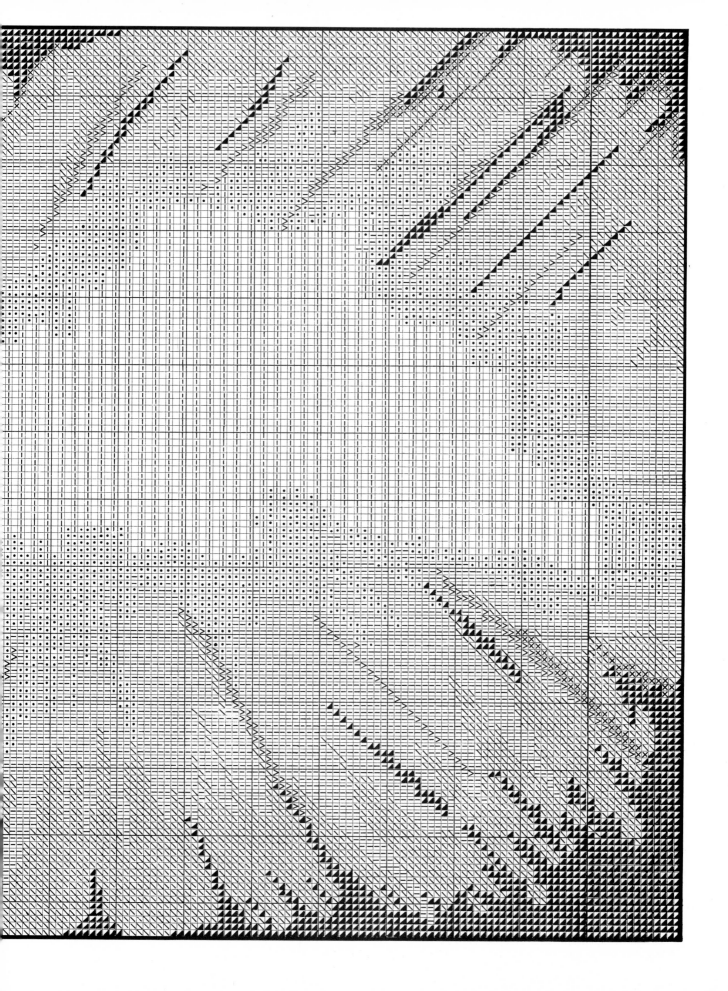

BOWKNOT RUG

Double bowknots, bold and handsome, pattern a latch hook rug inspired by a handwoven coverlet that was loomed in Ohio around 1867.

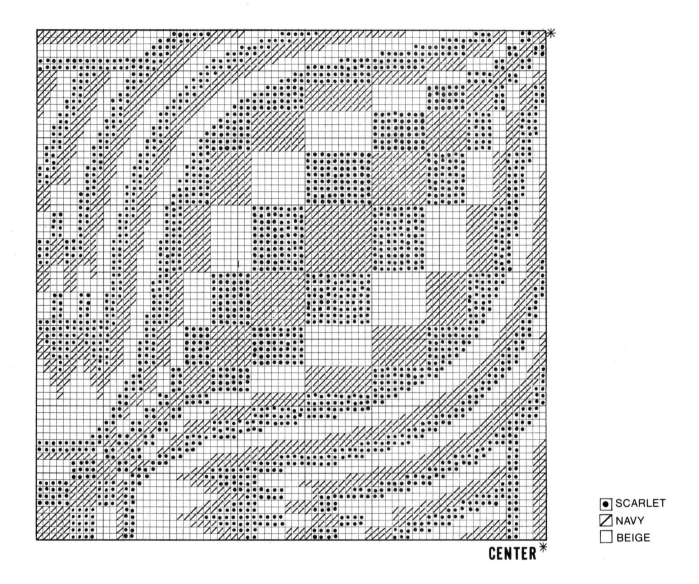

●	SCARLET
⟋	NAVY
☐	BEIGE

CENTER *

SIZE: 45″ x 41½″.

EQUIPMENT: Pencil. Latch (latchet) hook. Scissors.

MATERIALS: Precut turkey rug wool: scarlet, 30 packs; 24 packs each of beige and navy. Rug canvas, 3⅓ mesh to the inch, 45″ wide, 1½ yds.

DIRECTIONS: Read general directions on page 39. Rug chart, which is one-quarter of complete design, is 76 squares wide and 76 squares long. On one cut edge of canvas, mark the center. Chart is to be worked twice across canvas (from selvage to selvage), and twice along length. The design area will not quite be square because the canvas is not perfectly square.

Lay the canvas on table, with selvage edges at sides and about 2″ of canvas extending off the table toward you. Turn under four rows of the extended edge of canvas; work through this doubled canvas to form a finished end. Each square on chart represents one knot on canvas. Work the first row of knots from center to left edge. Continue to work across in rows from right (center) to left edge until one-quarter is completed. For second quarter, repeat chart in reverse, omitting center starred vertical row. For second half of rug, repeat design in reverse, omitting center starred horizontal row. Before reaching end, fold canvas under and work last four rows through doubled canvas as you did at the start. Trim off excess canvas on wrong side.

Finish according to directions on page 40.

DESIGN-A-RUG MOTIFS

Tricolor motifs for a rug: Combine them to make a rug the size and color to fit your decorating scheme. The 7″ motif shown is worked in red, white, and black, with six motif variations suggested. Choose three colors and a design, using one or a combination of the motifs and arranging them in a pattern as suggested below.

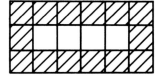 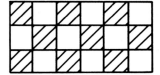 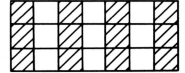 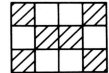

EQUIPMENT: Latch (latchet) hook. Scissors. Large sewing needle. Soft black pencil.

MATERIALS: Precut rug wool, 1-oz. unit packs, in three colors. Rug canvas, 4 mesh to the inch, 37″ or 61″ wide. Rug binding. Carpet thread.

DIRECTIONS: Motifs may be made 7″ square, as shown on opposite page, or 14″ square, as shown by graph charts on page 96. To work 7″-square motifs from the charts, a block of four squares of the graph represents one stitch on the canvas. To make 14″-square motifs, each square of graph represents one stitch on the canvas.

Plan rug design, using block motifs shown on page 96, to make rug of desired length and width. Selvage edges of canvas are sides of rug. Use combinations of pattern blocks, or combinations of plain and pattern blocks as shown above. Mark off the canvas in 7″ or 14″ square blocks with soft pencil, for a combination of plain and pattern blocks. For a rug of solid pattern blocks, use the border of one block as the border of adjacent blocks also, in order to keep the width of the borders equal between blocks and at outer edges.

Read general directions on page 39. Work each row of knots across canvas from right to left, or left to right, whichever seems more convenient; follow charts for block designs. To start rug, turn 1″ of canvas over to front, matching meshes, and work knots through double canvas for four rows, to make finished edge. Work remainder of rug through single canvas up to last four rows of design on chart. Cut off canvas beyond eight rows; turn four rows of canvas over to front and work last four rows through double canvas. Shake rug well and clip any long ends of yarn to make even pile.

Turn selvage edges of canvas to back and slipstitch to back of rug with carpet thread. Sew rug binding to back over selvage edges, stitching along both edges of binding with carpet thread. Finish according to directions on page 40.

4

Braided Rugs

The first braided rugs were made of rushes, plaited by the Egyptians as early as 6000 B.C. In similar fashion, the earliest American colonists covered their floors with braided cornhusk mats. Later the practical and inventive settlers learned to braid rags into durable and colorful rugs—and thus developed an apparently native American craft. Braided rugs are popular today—adding a casual charm and cheerful warmth to many styles of decor.

general directions

MATERIALS: Start planning for your rug in the old-fashioned way by collecting worn-out clothing in a ragbag. You may also buy material from remnant counters and mill-end shops. Generally, wool makes the best rugs; it works up easily, wears well, and shows less soil. Rugs may be braided with a variety of fabrics, but if different types of fabric are combined in a single rug they will wear unevenly. Cotton does not wear as well as wool and soils quickly, but it is inexpensive and easily washed. Silks and synthetics, such as old neckties and stockings, might be used for small bedroom rugs or for chair mats not subject to a great deal of wear.

Estimating Amount of Material: Plan the color scheme and the approximate amount and placement of each color before starting to braid. A woolen rug of average thickness requires about ¾ lb. of material for each square foot, so that a 2 x 3 ft. rug will take 4 to 5 lbs. When the desired color is not available, the fabric may be dyed (see page 166). All fabrics should be washed, each color separately, in warm water with borax or naphtha soap, rinsed without wringing, and hung in sunlight to dry. This helps to insure colorfastness and washability.

SIZE AND SHAPE: Make your rug in any size and shape suitable for the area in which it will be used. It may be scatter size or room size, rounded or rectangular. Examples of traditional shapes are shown at right and on following page. In oval and rectangular rugs the most pleasing proportions have proved

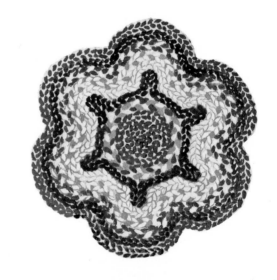

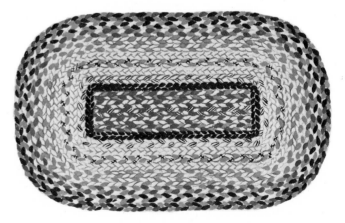

to be 2 x 3, 3 x 6, 4 x 7, 8 x 10, and 9 x 12 feet. The size must be decided before you start any shape other than round, for the starting braid will determine the finished rug size. To find the proper length for the starting braid of an oval rug, subtract the width of the desired size of the finished rug from the length. Example: To make a rug 38″ x 26″, start with a 12″-long braid in the center.

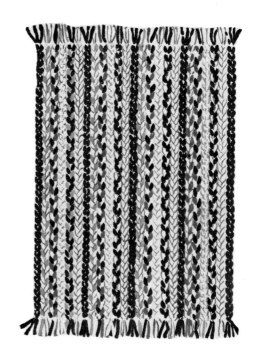

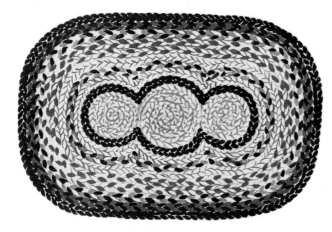

PREPARING STRIPS: Cut or tear strips on the lengthwise grain of fabric, the width determined by the weight of the fabric in relation to the thickness of the braid. For a large wool rug the finished braid is usually ¾″ or 1″ wide. The cut strip, therefore, should be 1½″ to 2″ wide for medium-weight wool. To make strips desired length, join pieces by sewing together on the bias by hand or machine. Start with strips of different lengths in order to avoid joinings all in the same place.

Strips made of firm, nonfraying cotton may also be spliced. Splicing is a simplified method of joining braiding strips to eliminate having to sew strips together. It does not make as smooth a braid as sewn strips, but it is quick and simple to do. Cut a 1″ slit lengthwise in the end of each strip. Pass slit end of strip being braided through slit of new strip. Pass other end of new strip through slit of strip being braided. Pull together (Fig. 1).

To gauge the amount of stripping needed, estimate the desired length of the finished braid and multiply by 1½. Prepare the strips for braiding by folding in the raw edges so that they almost meet at center, then fold the strip in half lengthwise. This may be done by hand as you braid or by using braiding aids (Fig. 3) that fold the strip automatically.

THREE-STRAND BRAID: The simplest type of braid is made with three strands. Pin or sew ends of three folded strands together. Anchor ends firmly (Fig. 2). Begin braiding by folding right-hand strand over middle strand, then fold left-hand strand over middle strand, keeping folded-in edges to center. Continue braiding, always folding alternate outside strand over middle strand (Fig. 2).

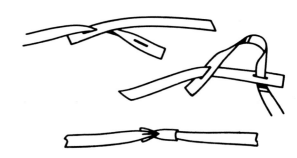

figure 1: THREE STEPS IN SPLICING

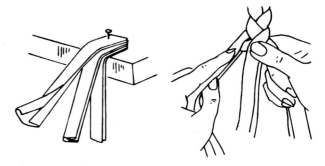

figure 2: STARTING A THREE-STRAND BRAID

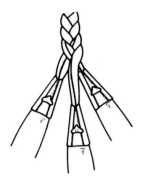

figure 3: RUG BRAIDERS FOR FOLDING STRIPS

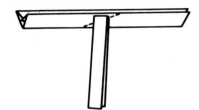

figure 4: STARTING A ROPE BRAID

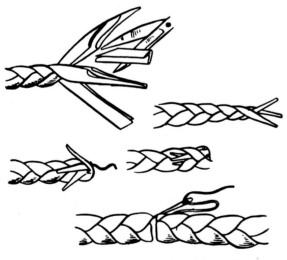

figure 5: FOUR STEPS IN BUTTING

figure 6: JOINING BY SEWING

SPIRAL ROUNDS: Braid may be made in a continuous rope and wound spirally in a round or oval shape. Start a continuous rope braid with a finished end. Select your three strips and sew the ends of two of these together with a bias seam; trim off corners of strips and press seam flat. Fold joined strip in half lengthwise with edges tucked in to center. Lay joined strip out horizontally with opening of fold at top. Fold in the end of third strip, fold strip in half lengthwise with edges tucked in, and sew end to first strips at point of joining, with opening of fold to the right (Fig. 4). Anchor end by pinning or nailing to a surface at joinihg to hold firmly. Braid as directed above.

For a continuous braid the changes in color combinations are usually made one strip at a time, at staggered intervals, to achieve a gradual blending of color. Sew or lace the continuous rounds of braid together until desired size is reached. The ending may come at any convenient point; if the rug is oval, it will usually be more satisfactory to end around a curve. Taper-trim each strip to a bias cut about 6″ long; braid right to the end, making the tail end very small. Sew tapered end in place along edge, tuck in tail end of braid through a loop of adjoining braid, and sew securely.

BUTTED ROUNDS: Many rugmakers prefer to butt each round. Butting is used to form a perfect circle, oval, or square, or to make sharp color changes. It eliminates the jogging-out of the pattern. Leave both ends of the braid unfinished. Sew braid to rug within 6″ of the point of butting. Cut strips of both unfinished ends diagonally, tapering to a point. Braid strips almost to end. Fold points of strips to back of braid and tuck neatly underneath the loops; spread braid to normal width, keeping square at end for neat joining. Sew finished ends together (Fig. 5). If braids are butted at different joints the joinings will be unnoticeable.

JOINING BRAIDS: Braids can be sewn together through adjacent edges with doubled heavy carpet thread, or laced through the braid loops. Work on a flat surface to keep rug flat and even. When sewing, take stitches at center sides of braids, using a curved upholstery needle (Fig. 6). To lace, fasten doubled carpet thread to a loop in braid on right, using blunt needle or lacer; push needle through loop of adjacent braid, then into next loop of first braid. Pull thread tightly to lock loops into each other, keeping thread invisible so that rug will be reversible.

DOUBLE LACING: For a rectangular rug of straight strips we recommend double lacing as the strongest joining. To double lace, fasten carpet thread to loop #1 of first braid with a darning needle, then replace needle with a lacer. Fasten a second piece of carpet thread to loop #3 of first braid, replace needle with second lacer. With first lacer go through loop #2 on second braid from center out, and down through loop #5. Lay first lacer on table above braids, at left. With second lacer go through loop #4 on second braid from center out, and down through loop #7, thus crossing threads between braids. Lay second lacer above braids at left. Pull threads tight. Continue in this manner to end of braids (Fig. 7). Lace another braid to other side of first braid in same manner. Keep center braid straight and continue to lace braids at both sides of center. To keep braids perfectly straight and evenly laced, attach center braid to wooden surface, such as plywood, with thin nails, stretching braid enough to keep work taut; fasten at ends and at equal intervals along braid. Continue lacing braids to each side and fasten a braid to board again after about six rows. When all braids are laced together, steam-press before removing nails.

FRINGING: If you wish to fringe the ends of a rectangular braided rug, make each braid the length of rug desired; hold each end with safety pin as strips are sewn together. When rug is complete, sew across ends of rug at point where you wish fringe to begin. Unravel ends of braids and trim evenly (Fig. 8).

FOUR-STRAND BRAID: In four-strand braiding the outer left-hand strand is carried each time over the next strand, under the following strand, and over the opposite outside strand (Fig. 9).

FIVE-STRAND BRAID: For a five-strand braid, it may help to baste the folded strands for ease in handling. Pin the five folded strands together. With folded-in edges to the left, anchor end firmly. In your mind, number strands 1 to 5 from left to right. Fold 1 over 2, put it under 3, over 4, under 5, folding 5 over 1 for a smooth edge. Strand 2 now becomes strand 1; continue in same manner, always weaving strand farthest to left over and under to right (Fig. 10).

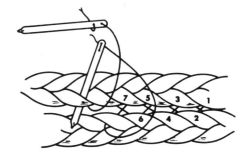

figure 7: JOINING BY DOUBLE LACING

figure 8: FRINGING A STRIPED RUG

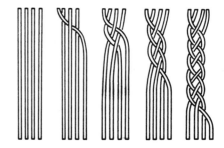

figure 9: FOUR-STRAND BRAIDING

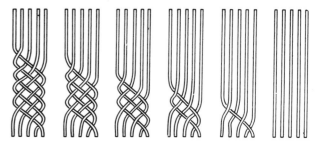

figure 10: FIVE-STRAND BRAIDING

RECTANGULAR RUG

This beautiful, warmly colored rug is made in an unusual rectangular shape, combining five-strand braids in the center with three-strand braids in a wide border.

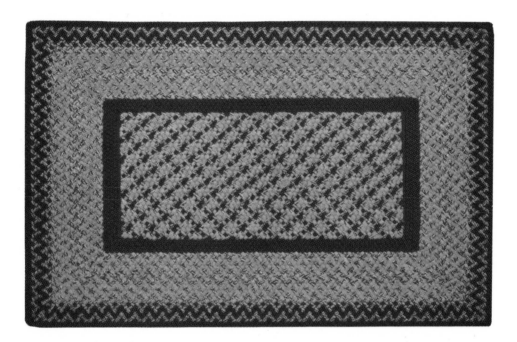

SIZE: 30" x 45½".

EQUIPMENT: Large upholstery needle or lacers. Scissors. Tape measure. Rug braiders (optional).

MATERIALS: About 7½ lbs. medium-weight wool fabrics: pink, brown-and-white check, and brown. Heavy brown carpet thread.

DIRECTIONS: Read general directions on pages 97–100. Center of rug is five-strand braids 1¼" wide; wide border is three-strand braids ¾" wide. Cut fabric 1¼" to 1½" wide. Sew strips together, using one color for each strand.

Center: Place five strands for first braid on pin, with folded-in edges to left as follows: two strands pink, one strand brown-and-white check. Make 30" five-strand braid as directed on page 100. Make ten more braids same length, changing color sequence on pins by shifting strands one color over to the right for each successive braid. To lace braids together, place braids with starting pins pointing downward to right and folded-in edges upward. Match colors of first and second braids; attach thread to end loop of second braid, push lacer up into matching loop of first braid, down into next loop of second braid, and continue. Lace third braid to second, etc. When

braids are all joined, stitch straight across each end, remove pins, cut away fabric outside stitching. Bind ends with a 1¼" strip of brown.

Border: Start making three-strand braid in brown, 2" shorter than length of one side of center section. Turn center to wrong side, lace braid just made along right-hand edge, starting 2" from bottom, with folded-in edges of braid facing up. Turn work around and braid corner as follows: place left strand 1 over 2, 2 over 1, 1 over 2 again; pull strand 3 very tight and braid in usual way. Make all corners the same. Sew braid to bound ends of center. Butt ends of braid together. Make one more brown round same. For border, put folded strands of wool on pin as follows: **Round 3:** two brown-and-white, one pink. **Rounds 4 and 5:** two pink, one brown-and-white. **Rounds 6 and 7:** two brown-and-white, one pink. **Rounds 8 and 9:** two pink, one brown-and-white. **Round 10:** two brown-and-white, one pink. **Round 11:** two brown-and-white, one brown. **Round 12:** two brown, one brown-and-white. **Round 13:** two brown-and-white, one brown. **Rounds 14 and 15:** three brown. Turn corners; butt ends of each round.

OVAL RUG

Rich hues are used for this stunning rug, made with butted rounds of three-strand braids in a classic oval.

SIZE: 42″ x 60″.

EQUIPMENT: Large upholstery needle or lacers. Scissors. Tape measure. Rug braiders (optional).

MATERIALS (approx.): Medium-weight wool fabrics; 2½ lbs. each golden yellow, orange, bright maroon-red; 2 lbs. green; 4 lbs. blue. Heavy thread.

DIRECTIONS: Read general directions pages 97–100. Rug is made of ¾″-wide braids. Experiment with fabric to see how wide you must cut the strips to obtain an even ¾″-wide braid throughout the rug. Start with a golden yellow braid 42″ long (**Round 1**). Fold braid in half; butt the ends neatly and sew inner edges of braid together. Make each braid in succeedingly longer lengths, and butt each round. Be sure to allow enough length in each braid to ease around curves at each end in order to keep the rug flat. Do not cut off fabric strips of braids until making butt joint.

To form the pattern shown, make three-strand braids, using colors for each strand of each round as follows. (**Note:** Y is golden yellow; OR is orange; R is bright maroon-red; G is green; B is blue.) **Round 1:** 3 Y. **Round 2:** 2 Y, 1 OR. **Round 3:** 2 OR, 1 Y. **Round 4:** 1 R, 1 OR, 1 Y. **Round 5:** 2 R, 1 OR. **Round 6:** 3 R. **Round 7:** 2 G, 1 B. **Round 8:** 3 B. **Round 9:** 2 G, 1 B. **Round 10:** 3 Y. **Round 11:** 2 Y, 1 OR. **Round 12:** 2 OR, 1 Y. **Round 13:** 3 OR. **Round 14:** 2 R, 1 OR. **Round 15:** 3 R. **Round 16:** 2 G, 1 B. **Round 17:** 3 B. **Round 18:** 2 G, 1 B. **Round 19:** 3 Y. **Round 20:** 2 Y, 1 OR. **Round 21:** 3 OR. **Round 22:** 1 R, 1 OR, 1 Y. **Round 23:** 2 R, 1 OR. **Round 24:** 3 R. **Round 25:** 2 G, 1 B. **Round 26:** 3 B. **Round 27;** 2 G, 1 B. **Round 28:** 3 B. **Round 29:** 3 B.

SPIRALED CAT RUG

Sew multicolor braids in two spiral circles for a whimsical "calico" cat rug! Features are felt, with embroidered whiskers.

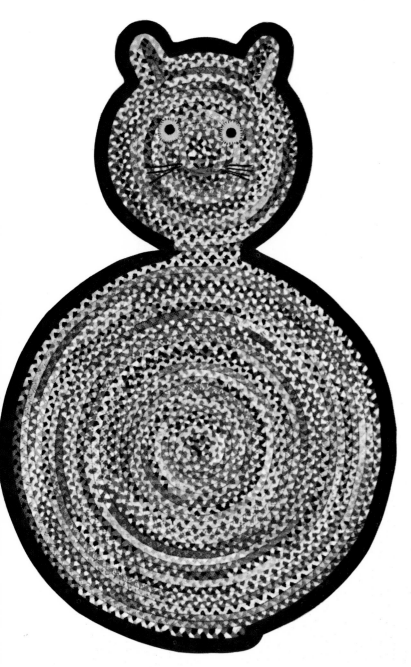

SIZE: 32" x 52".

EQUIPMENT: Large upholstery needle or lacers. Scissors. Tape measure. Rug braiders (optional).

MATERIALS: About 6 lbs. medium-weight wool fabrics, all colors. Black carpet thread. Scraps of blue, black, and red felt. Black embroidery cotton.

DIRECTIONS: Read general directions on pages 97–100. The three-strand braids are ¾" wide. Experiment to determine width that strips should be cut to make braid this size. Start braiding with uneven lengths in order to avoid joining all strips in same place. Add colors as each strip ends, taking care to harmonize colors within one braid. One strip of black in a braid has been used profusely; outline picks up the black.

Body: Start at center, sewing braids in a spiral. Attach pin at one point to mark neck center. Make 26 rounds, widening braid opposite pin for tail.

Head: With another braid, start head, working in a spiral. Make 11 rounds, attaching a pin at one point to mark neck center. On twelfth round, shape ears opposite pin by attaching projecting doubled braids 3½" long, placing them 6" apart. On outside of each ear add a 3" braid. Thirteenth round follows shape and ends at base of one ear. Add a 5½" braid to fit between ears and two 5¼" braids, each centered on pinned edge of head and body; join these two.

Finish with two black rounds, butting each round.

Face: Cut two light-blue felt circular eye pieces 2" across, tapering one section of each piece to a point; cut two ¾" black circles. Sew black circles to centers of eyes. From red felt, cut an oval nose ¾" long, ¼" wide, and a curved mouth with pointed ends 1" wide at center, 3" long. Sew features to face with black cotton, taking over-and-over stitches ⅛" apart. Sew eyes 3" apart, points toward center, above center of head. Sew nose just below center. Sew mouth below nose. Embroider black whiskers in outline stitch.

5

Needlepoint Rugs

Needlepoint rugs today are most often worked on large-mesh canvas in a method referred to as "quick point." Regardless of the size of the canvas, the needlepoint stitches are always worked the same. Traditional rugs, stitched on a finer canvas, are included here as well as the modern adaptations.

general directions

MATERIALS AND EQUIPMENT: Needlepoint rugs are usually worked in rug wool or two or more strands of tapestry wool. Double-mesh canvases range from 3⅓, 4, or 5 meshes to the inch and come in widths from 14″ to 80″. Buy canvas with a regular mesh and no weak or tied threads; it should have a glossy finish, as the coating adds strength. If possible, use wool and canvas made by the same manufacturer for each rug, as they will be coordinated in size. A large-eyed rug (tapestry) needle with a blunt point is used; it should have an eye large enough to accommodate the yarn, but not larger than needed. The rug may be worked on a frame or not, as desired.

TO WORK NEEDLEPOINT: The selvage edges of canvas are the sides of rug. Mark top with a colored thread. Allow at least a 2″ margin of plain canvas at top and bottom of rug and at sides if selvages have been cut off. Before beginning, bind all raw edges of canvas, using masking tape, adhesive tape, or a double-fold bias binding; or turn raw edges to back and whipstitch in place. Needlepoint rugs are worked from top to bottom. When the needlepoint is completed and blocked, edges are finished (see page 106). If desired, top and bottom edges can be finished while working needlepoint. Trim top margin of canvas to 1″, turn to back, and baste in place. Work beginning of rug through double thickness of canvas. When 1″ from end of rug design, trim canvas to 2″, turn 1″ to back, and baste in place. Work bottom of rug through double thickness. If planning to work an edge stitch (see below) all around rug, leave a double-thread edge of canvas free at top and bottom of rug.

Use either the diagonal or continental method of working basic needlepoint stitch; details are on page 106. The diagonal method will provide a heavier backing for the rug than the continental method. Designs in this book are given in chart form; each square on the chart equals one mesh on the canvas. Start design at upper right-hand corner. When working in diagonal stitch, work background to beginning of design area. Work design area, following chart and filling in background as you go.

Cut yarn strands into 18″ lengths (do not break yarn, as this will stretch it): To thread yarn, double it over the end of the needle and slip it off, holding it tightly as close as possible to the fold. Push the flattened, folded end through the needle eye and pull yarn through. To start, leave 1″ end of yarn at back of canvas and cover this as work proceeds. Work needlepoint in specified stitch, being careful not to pull yarn too tightly. Hold thumb on yarn near stitch until you have pulled yarn through the canvas, then lift thumb and pull yarn gently into place. Keep yarn from twisting to avoid thin places in work, letting it drop now and then to untwist. When close to the end of a strand, fasten yarn by weaving through a few stitches on back of work. Immediately clip ends close, to avoid tangles. When a mistake is made, pluck out yarn with blunt end of needle, or run needle under stitch and snip yarn with embroidery scissors close to needle. Do not reuse pulled-out yarn. If not using a frame, roll canvas as you work, from the bottom up or the top down, for ease in handling.

A large rug may be worked in sections (see "Joining Canvas," page 163).

BLOCKING: Rugs must be blocked if they have been pulled out of shape when worked. If rug has become soiled, first brush over the surface with a clean cloth dipped in carbon tetrachloride or other cleaning fluid. Colors will brighten and return to their original look. No matter how badly a piece is pulled out of shape, it may be blocked squarely. Cover a soft wooden surface with brown paper. Mark on this the size of canvas, being sure that corners are square. Place smooth-surface needlepoint right side down over the guide; if rug has been worked with tufted or raised stitches to give texture, piece should be blocked right side up. Fasten with thumbtacks about ½″ or ¾″ apart along the edge of the canvas. Wet thoroughly with cold water; let dry. (If yarn is not colorfast, apply solution of salt and water generously to needlepoint.) If work is badly warped, restretch, wet, and dry again.

TO FINISH EDGES: Trim margin of canvas to 1″; turn margin under and baste to back of rug. If using an edging stitch, leave a double-thread edge of canvas free at edges of rug. Cut off part of corners diagonally; miter corners to make them lie flat. Rug may be finished in one of several ways:

Rug Binding: With wrong side of rug facing you, sew one edge of rug binding along folded edge of canvas; sew other edge of binding to back of rug, covering raw edges of canvas; miter. Keep binding loose.

Lining: Cut lining same size as rug, excluding any fringe, plus 1″ all around. Turn under 1″ margin; miter corners, trim, and slip-stitch. With carpet thread, slip-stitch lining to rug.

Edging Stitch: One of two edging stitches may be used: (1) Work over double-thread edge in a whipstitch, making one stitch in the mesh and one stitch between the threads, to cover canvas. (2) Work plaited edge stitch (see details on page 162). After the edging stitch is worked, rug may be finished with rug binding or a lining, if desired.

To reduce wear, rug may be placed on a rug pad cut to size slightly smaller than rug.

needlepoint stitches

Continental Stitch

Start design at upper right corner. To begin, hold an inch of yarn in back and work over this end. All other strands may be started and finished by running them through wrong side of finished work. Details 1 and 2 show placement and direction of needle; turn work around for return row. Detail 1 shows starting new row below finished portion. Detail 2 shows starting a new row above finished portion. Always work from right to left. Finish design, then fill in background.

Diagonal Stitch (Basketweave)

Begin by tying a knot at end of yarn and putting needle through canvas to back, diagonally down from upper right-hand corner of work. Never turn work; hold it in the same position. Step 1: The knot is on top. Bring needle up at A, down through B and out through C. Step 2: Needle in D, out through E. Step 3: Needle in F, out through G. Step 4: Start next row in at H and out through I.

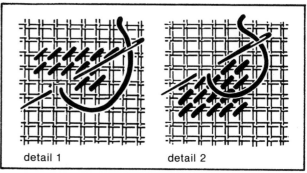

CONTINENTAL STITCH

detail 1   detail 2

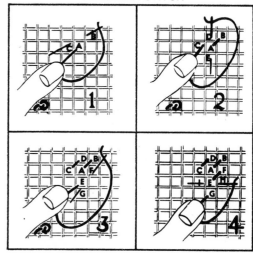

DIAGONAL STITCH

1   2

3   4

You are now ready to work from the big diagram. Each stitch is drawn on big diagram with blunt and point ends. Put needle in at pointed end and out at blunt end.

Stitch No. 5 is your next stitch. It extends from space I to A. Complete the stitches to 10 on diagram in numerical order to finish the diagonal row. Stitch No. 11 starts the next row diagonally upward.

After starting row going up, needle is horizontal. Needle slants diagonally to begin new row down, as in Step 1. Going down, needle is always vertical, as in Step 2; and again, when the last stitch is made, the needle slants diagonally to begin next row up, Step 3.

Work as far as knot; cut off. All other strands of yarn may be started and ended by running them through the finished work on the back. Work background to design; work design. Finish background.

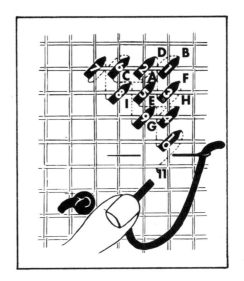

pattern stitches

When choosing a pattern stitch, experiment with yarn and canvas before starting rug, making sure that yarn covers canvas well. Usually rugs are made with rug yarn or two or more strands of tapestry yarn; however, most stitches here were worked with one strand of tapestry yarn, to show details clearly. Be sure stitches have no long, easily snagged strands.

Mosaic Stitch

Consists of long and short stitches taken alternately in diagonal rows. Insert the needle one mesh to the right, going up one mesh for a short stitch and two meshes for a long stitch. In each succeeding row, a short stitch is worked into the end of a long stitch and a long stitch into the end of a short stitch.

Hungarian Stitch

Starting at the left, work upright stitches—the first stitch over two meshes, the second stitch over four meshes, and the third stitch over two meshes, making a diamond shape. Skip one vertical mesh and repeat; continue across to the right. On second row, work a longer center stitch in open mesh between diamonds of first row, using second color if desired.

MOSAIC STITCH

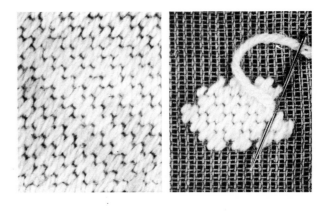

HUNGARIAN STITCH

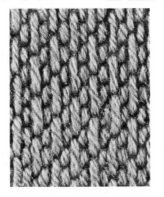

Rice Stitch

Working from left to right, make the bottom half of crosses diagonally over two meshes to the right. Return to left, making top half of crosses diagonally to the left. Using a finer yarn, take a small diagonal stitch over each arm of crosses, having the stitches meet in the meshes between the arms of the crosses.

Jacquard Stitch

Starting at the upper left, work diagonal stitches over two horizontal and two vertical meshes of canvas. Make six stitches down, then six stitches to right; continue down and across for desired length. For next row to right, work diagonal stitches over one mesh of canvas, making same number of stitches down and across. Repeat these two rows alternately.

Interlocking Gobelin

This is a very easy stitch that works up quickly. Work back and forth in horizontal rows, from left to right, and from right to left. To start, bring needle to front of canvas; make first stitch two meshes up and one mesh over (half of a cross-stitch). Continue making stitches in each mesh across canvas. At end of row, bring needle out one mesh below. Make same stitch reversed, like second half of cross, inserting needle one mesh above bottom of the last row, thus interlocking the end of the stitch. Continue across row. Always start the next row one mesh below last.

Soumack Stitch (Knitting Stitch)

This is a good background stitch that covers the canvas well. Work each row from right to left. Bring needle up between double strands of a horizontal row of canvas. Two meshes to the right, bring yarn under the same row, working through a mesh above and below. Insert needle between strands of same row in same place as beginning of stitch. To start next stitch, bring needle out between strands of same row, one mesh to left. Make stitch under same row, one mesh to the left of the first stitch. Continue across (see detail). End thread. Make next row above or below, in same way.

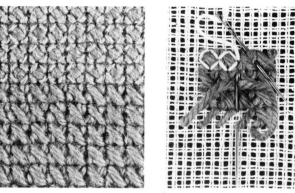

RICE STITCH

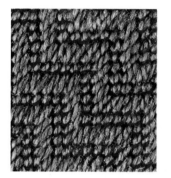

JACQUARD STITCH

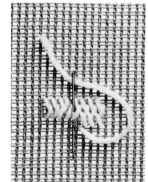

INTERLOCKING GOBELIN

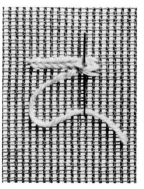

SOUMACK STITCH

Greek Stitch

Start in fourth mesh below top left corner of area to be embroidered. Insert needle at top, into fourth mesh from corner; bring out in corner (Fig. 1).

At bottom of row, insert needle in seventh mesh from left side; bring to front in fourth mesh from left (Fig. 2).

At top of row, insert needle three meshes to right of completed stitch; bring out in same mesh as last stitch completed (Fig. 3).

At bottom of row, insert needle three meshes to right of completed stitch; bring out in same mesh as last stitch completed (Fig. 4). Continue across. See Figs. 3 and 4.

To start next row, begin three meshes below worked row (upper part of stitches will be in same meshes as bottom of stitches of last row).

GREEK STITCH

Figure 1

Figure 2

Figure 3

Figure 4

Ghiordes (Turkey) Knot

This loop stitch forms a good pile for a complete rug, or it may be used in combination with another stitch. Cut the loops after working each row if cut loops are desired. Work from left to right only. Insert needle between strands of a double vertical row of canvas and out through mesh at left; leave yarn end on front of canvas. With yarn above row, insert needle in mesh to right and out between same strands to left; pull stitch tight. With yarn below row, insert needle between next two vertical strands to right and out in mesh to left; pull yarn through, leaving a loop below row. Insert needle in mesh to right and out between same strands to left (see detail). Continue in this manner across.

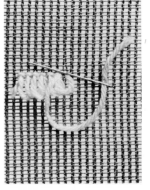

GHIORDES STITCH

French Stitch

Makes a flat, interesting texture, which is good for backgrounds. Work the stitch diagonally up or down, and from left to right. It consists of two horizontal stitches made in same mesh, couched with two vertical stitches at center.

Bring needle to front of canvas through one mesh, down through fifth mesh to right and out to front again in mesh above at center (Fig. 1). Pull into place.

Make vertical stitch, inserting needle in center mesh of same row as horizontal stitch; bring needle out in same mesh as beginning (Fig. 2).

Make another horizontal stitch same as first one; bring needle out one mesh below at center (Fig. 3).

Make vertical stitch, inserting needle in same center mesh as first; to start next stitch diagonally to right, bring needle out in same mesh as bottom vertical stitch (Fig. 4). Continue in same manner, making diagonal rows from top to bottom.

When the long diagonal rows are completed, fill in the remaining areas with the same stitch as above.

FRENCH STITCH

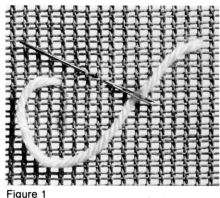

Figure 1

Figure 2

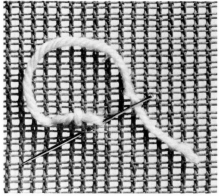

Figure 3

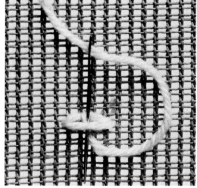

Figure 4

GREEK THISTLE RUG

Thistles in rows make a versatile pattern on this rug from Greece. Worked in the herringbone stitch, a variation of the continental stitch, the rug can be made to any size you wish, simply by repeating the motif out to any side.

EQUIPMENT: Ruler. Indelible waterproof felt-tipped pen in a light color. Large-eyed tapestry needle. Scissors. Sewing needle. Masking tape. **For Blocking:** Soft wooden surface. Brown wrapping paper. Rustproof thumbtacks. Square. Pencil.

MATERIALS (for amounts, see table): Tapestry wool, 100-yd. or 40-yd. skeins: dark rose, golden bronze, blue, fern green, olive green, off-white. Double-mesh needlepoint canvas, 10 mesh to the inch. Carpet thread.

DIRECTIONS: Read general directions on page 105. Directions are given so that rug can be made up in one of four different sizes. Refer to table for yarn amounts and size of canvas for size rug desired. Amounts are given in yardage; to find number of 40-yd. or 100-yd. skeins required, divide yardage by 40 or 100, whichever is suitable.

The table indicates the number of large and small motifs and includes yarn amounts for all motifs, border, and background color. When working any of the three larger sizes, it will be necessary to piece the canvas to obtain the correct size. See "Joining Canvas," on page 163.

First, plan the placement and number of motifs and the border. Using indelible pen and leaving a 2" margin on each side, mark outline of finished size on canvas. Mark 4" border all around. Referring to table, divide the inside space into the number of rectangles required for large motifs. Large motifs measure 6" x 9", and are spaced 6 rows apart in each direction. There are 4 rows between border and large motifs. Place a small motif in each space between four large motifs, centering them where the marked lines intersect. Chart on opposite page shows one corner of rug and includes border, one large motif, and one small motif; chart also indicates placement of motifs in relation to each other.

Rug as shown was worked entirely in a variation of the continental stitch, in which the direction of stitches alternates in each row (see stitch detail below). This produces a herringbone effect. However, the entire rug may be worked in regular continental stitch if desired (see page 106). Follow chart and color key to work design.

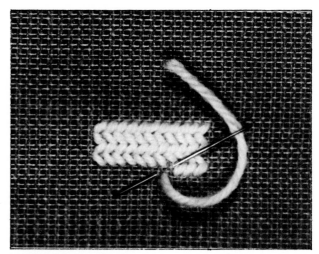

HERRINGBONE STITCH

Begin working at upper right corner of canvas, with the selvages of the canvas at the sides as you work. Following chart, work the large motifs first, centering them in the marked rectangles. Then work small motifs between them. Work border next, following the leaves and border stripes as given in chart and repeating them all around. Fill in the background last.

When rug is complete, block as directed on page 106. Finish edges as desired; see page 161.

YARDAGE TABLE

Finished Size	Canvas Size	Number of Large Motifs	Number of Small Motifs	YARN AMOUNTS IN YARDAGE (including borders)					
				Dark Rose	Bronze	Blue	Fern Green	Olive Green	Off-White
28" x 28"	32" x 32"	6	2	21 yds.	7 yds.	13 yds.	126 yds.	264 yds.	574 yds.
28" x 48"	32" x 52"	12	6	42 yds.	13 yds.	28 yds.	200 yds.	407 yds.	1,024 yds.
48" x 48"	52" x 52"	24	15	84 yds.	26 yds.	59 yds.	306 yds.	527 yds.	1,824 yds.
*48" x 67"	52" x 71"	36	24	125 yds.	37 yds.	79 yds.	376 yds.	767 yds.	2,587 yds.

*size shown

- ⊟ DARK ROSE
- ⧅ BLUE
- ⊠ OLIVE GREEN
- ⎅ GOLDEN BRONZE
- ⊡ FERN GREEN
- ☐ OFF-WHITE

STRAWBERRY RUG

A field of strawberries on an ivory ground makes a pretty accent rug. The Kalem stitch gives a knitted look to the surface.

SIZE: About 26″ x 37″.

EQUIPMENT: Tape measure. Scissors. Waterproof fine-tip felt marking pen in light color. Masking or adhesive tape. Ruler. Tapestry needles. Sewing needle. **For Blocking:** Soft wooden surface. Brown wrapping paper. Rustproof thumbtacks. Pencil. Square.

MATERIALS: Needlepoint canvas (mono or double mesh), 10 mesh to the inch, 34″ x 44″. (An ample amount of canvas is required because of the method of working the design.) Tapestry wool, 40-yd. or 100-yd. skeins: red, 1 100-yd., 1 40-yd; antique gold, 1 100-yd.; fern green, 1 100-yd., 1 40-yd.; light olive green, 3 100-yd.; ivory, 4 100-yd., 1 40-yd. White glue.

DIRECTIONS: Read general directions on page 105. Test marking pen for colorfastness. Along one crosswise (shorter) edge of canvas mark a line 2″ in from the taped edge. Find the center point of this line and mark it up the entire length of the canvas. These two lines will be the guidelines for placement of the needlepoint design.

The designs are made by repeating the charted motifs: Chart 1, border strawberry motif; Chart 2, main strawberry motif; and Chart 3, center border leaf motif.

Work with one strand of yarn in needle throughout; because of frequent color changes you may want to thread a needle with each color of yarn. Except for the outer edge, the rug is worked in a variation of Kalem stitch throughout. The Kalem stitch (Figs. 1-5) is worked vertically. Complete rug may be worked in continental stitch if desired.

Begin at center of crosswise edge. Align lengthwise canvas mark with vertical chart marks to work central motif of border. Then work strawberry border (Chart 1). Arrows indicate strawberry repeat; charted partial motifs are to clarify placement of full repeat motif. Work three border strawberry repeats out to each side (reverse direction of motifs on left of center) before stitching corner motifs. Working from the corners down each lengthwise edge, work six strawberry repeats, skip one canvas thread (which is the center of the edge), then work six repeats in opposite direction. Main rug design consists of five rows of three main strawberry motifs. Mark center crosswise line across the canvas along the skipped canvas thread. Match vertical and horizontal guidelines on Chart 2 to place main strawberry motif in the center on intersection of vertical and horizontal lines of canvas. Work center motif following chart. Space all repeats out from this center, keeping each four meshes apart from the next.

Complete border around all edges, then fill in background with ivory.

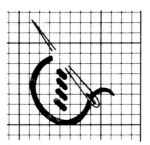
Figure 1

Figure 2

Figure 3

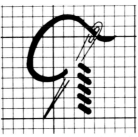

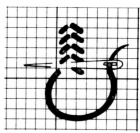

Figure 4   Figure 5

KALEM STITCH

When needlepoint is complete, block, following directions on page 106. Trim canvas margins to 1″. Finish with plaited edge stitch (see page 162).

If desired, coat wrong side of rug with a mixture of half white (Sobo) glue and half water. Brush on mixture, then let dry thoroughly.

Rug may also be lined. Cut lining same size as rug plus 1″ all around. Turn under 1″ margin; miter corners, trim, and slip-stitch. With carpet thread, slip-stitch to rug.

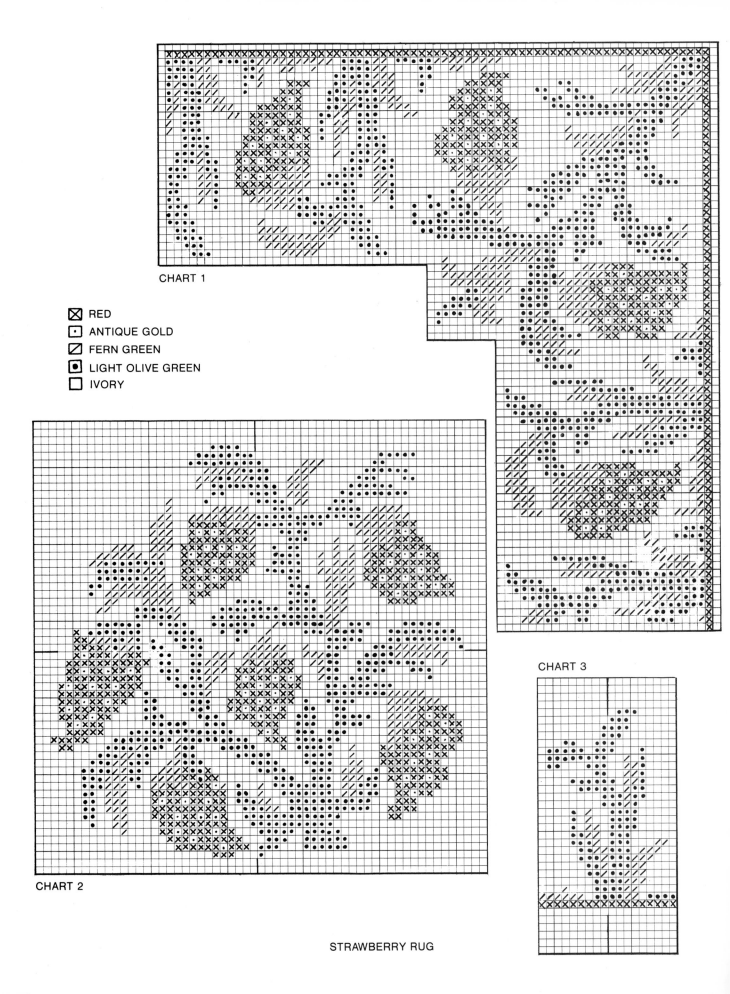

CHART 1

⊠ RED
⊡ ANTIQUE GOLD
⊘ FERN GREEN
⬤ LIGHT OLIVE GREEN
☐ IVORY

CHART 3

CHART 2

STRAWBERRY RUG

"AFGHAN" RUG

Brilliant diamonds, edged in black, give the effect of a crocheted granny afghan. The diamonds are worked in an up-and-down stitch with rug yarn, then interwoven with finer black yarn.

SIZE: 23" x 33" (without fringe).
EQUIPMENT: Pencil. Ruler. Masking tape. Large-eyed tapestry needle. Large-eyed sewing needle. Scissors. Crochet hook. Indelible waterproof felt-tipped pen in a light color. **For Blocking:** Rustproof thumbtacks. Square. Soft wooden surface. Brown wrapping paper. Pencil.
MATERIALS: Rug yarn: black, 8 ozs. (for outlining diamonds); assorted bright colors, totaling 1¾ lbs. Persian yarn: black, approx. 6 ozs. Double-thread, 4-mesh-to-the-inch canvas, 28" x 38½". Black carpet thread.
DIRECTIONS: Read general directions on page 105. Mark off design area on canvas 23" x 33", leaving a 2½" margin all around. Outline with thread or waterproof marking pen.

Rug yarn is used throughout except for black interwoven running stitch explained later. Cut strands as specified and work with yarn doubled. In order to avoid too many ends on back, cut strands in the following lengths: For outlining diamonds, black rug yarn in 2-yd. strands; for outer diamonds, 2-yd. strands; for middle diamonds, 1¼-yd. strands; and for inner diamonds, 18" to 20" strands. Save all end pieces for other inner diamonds, half diamonds, and fringe.

Work stitches vertically, each stitch starting one mesh up or down from previous stitch, always over two meshes. Begin at upper right-hand corner and refer to the color photograph for stitch count and color variations. Work black rug yarn, outlining diamonds first. Work diamond from outside to center.

When working to the marked outline, fill in with shorter stitches where necessary to make an even edge.

For running stitch, use 2-yd. strands of Persian yarn doubled over. Interweave straight across rug by going under center of each stitch, just catching yarn, not the canvas. To come across again, turn rug and interweave back. To end off, run yarn end under stitches on back of rug.

Block needlepoint and finish sides as directed on page 106.

For fringed ends, fold canvas under, one mesh beyond last row. With carpet thread, whipstitch margin to back. Cut 6" lengths of yarn, color matching to each stitch on last row; fold each in half. Using crochet hook, attach fringe as follows: Insert hook from top through back, hooking looped yarn and pulling through. Catch cut ends and pull through loop. Pull taut. Trim fringe ends evenly.

STRIPED RUG

The detail of the striped rug shows the stitches—the entire rug is worked in oblong cross-stitch with backstitch, in three colors: rose, gray and white. You can substitute any colors and achieve the same boldly appealing result.

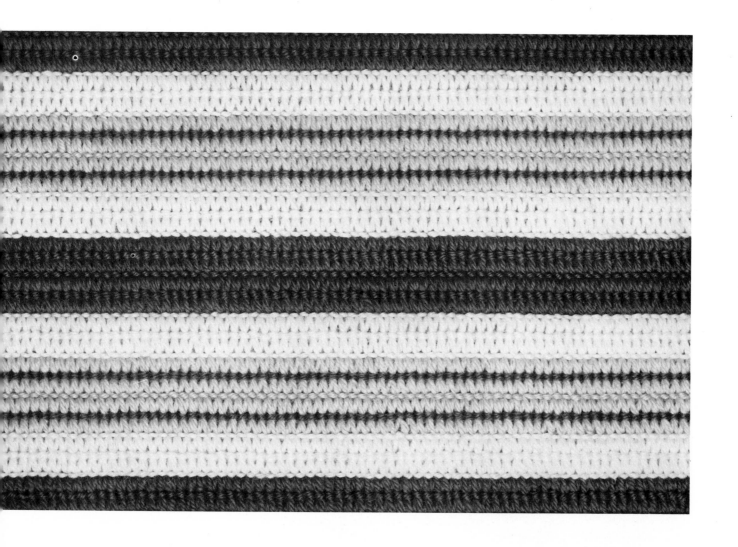

SIZE: 28" x 40".

EQUIPMENT: Large-eyed rug needle. Scissors. Ruler. Pencil. Sewing needle. Masking tape.

MATERIALS: Rug yarn, 1-oz. skeins: 12 dark rose, 7 gray, 9 white. Rug canvas, 4 mesh to the inch, 32" wide, 1¼ yds. Rug binding. Carpet thread.

DIRECTIONS: Read general directions on page 105. Turn canvas so that selvages are at top and bottom of width. Mark area 28" x 40" on canvas, leaving equal margins all around. Work entire rug area along length in rows of oblong cross-stitch (see stitch details at right): * 2 rows rose, 1 row white, 2 rows gray, 1 row white; repeat from * three times, add 2 rows rose. Backstitch over rose and gray cross-stitches with rose, over white cross-stitches with white. Backstitch between pairs of rose rows with rose, between pairs of gray rows with gray, each side of white rows with white yarn.

Block and finish edges as directed on page 106.

Oblong Cross-Stitch with Backstitch

Make the long cross-stitches over four horizontal meshes and one vertical mesh of the canvas. Starting at bottom left, make first half of each cross to right end of the row (Fig. 1). Work back to left, making second half of cross (Fig. 2). Over the center of each cross-stitch make a backstitch, going in and out of meshes at each side of cross (Fig. 3). Make tops and bottoms of each row of crosses in same meshes. Work row of backstitch between rows of crosses.

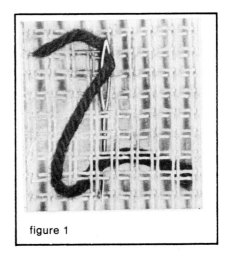

figure 1

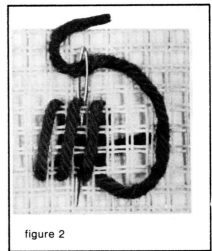

figure 2

figure 3

OBLONG CROSS-STITCH WITH BACKSTITCH

FOLK ART RUG

Playing children, birds, beasts, and flowers combine to make a charming rug—or wall hanging—for a child's room. The design was adapted from the three traditional Middle Eastern rugs shown, which suggest other motifs and borders for your own pattern.

SIZE: 29½" x 57".

EQUIPMENT: Masking tape, large-eyed tapestry needle. Scissors. Indelible waterproof felt-tipped pen in a light color. **For Blocking:** Rustproof thumbtacks. Soft wooden surface. Brown wrapping paper. Ruler. Square. Pencil.

MATERIALS: Rug yarn, 35-yd. skeins: lime green, 12 skeins; fir green, 5 skeins; emerald, 2 skeins; white, 2 skeins; yellow, 2 skeins; teal blue, 2 skeins; scarlet, 2 skeins; walnut, 2 skeins; medium orange, 2 skeins; royal blue, 2 skeins; salmon, 2 skeins. Rug canvas, 4 mesh to the inch, 36" wide, 1¾ yds. Carpet thread. White glue.

DIRECTIONS: Read general directions on page 105. Mark outline of rug 29½" x 57" on canvas, leaving about 3" margin all around. Outline with thread or waterproof marking pen. Use either continental or diagonal method of working needlepoint (see page 106). Start at upper right-hand corner of marked area on canvas. Follow illustration on pages 122 and 123 for design and colors. Work border for a short distance on top and sides; work motifs; then fill in background and finish the border. Block as instructed in general directions on page 106.

Finish sides as desired; see page 106. Make 10 tassels 3½" long, using all colors of yarn in each; see page 162 for method.

Make a twisted cord to fit around edges of rug, using three strands of lime green, each 14 yds. long (or make two cords, using yarn strands half this length); see page 162. Tie ends with thread. Sew twisted cord around edges through canvas. Tie tassels onto cord with top ends of tassel yarn; tape tie ends on back.

If desired, coat wrong side of rug with a mixture of half white (Sobo) glue and half water. Brush on mixture, then let dry thoroughly.

121

123

NURSERY RHYME RUG

Boys and girls join hands to go around the mulberry bush, monkeys and weasels "pop" from the corners in this delightful enactment of two nursery rhymes.

SIZE: 34" x 59".

EQUIPMENT: Large-eyed tapestry needle. Large-eyed rug needle. Scissors. Ruler. Masking tape. Soft pencil. **For Blocking:** Soft wooden surface. Brown wrapping paper. Rustproof thumbtacks. Square.

MATERIALS: Rug wool: cream, 33 skeins; bright green, 8 skeins; medium blue, 7 skeins; dark brown, 5 skeins; red, 5 skeins; pale pink, 2 skeins; golden orange, 3 skeins; black, 2 skeins; deep rose, 1 skein; bright yellow, 1 skein. Rug canvas, 5 mesh to the inch, 40" wide, 2 yds. Carpet thread.

DIRECTIONS: Read general directions on page 105. Mark working area of canvas 34" x 59", leaving 3" margins; cut off excess length. Bind raw edges.

Use either the diagonal or continental method for working needlepoint stitch (page 106). Work with one strand in the needle. Following chart on page 126 for one-quarter of rug, work border and design areas first, then continue to left side of canvas, working chart in reverse. For alternate corners, substitute the monkey in place of the weasel, following small chart. Repeat top half in reverse to complete rug. Then fill in background.

Block as instructed and finish as desired, according to directions on page 106.

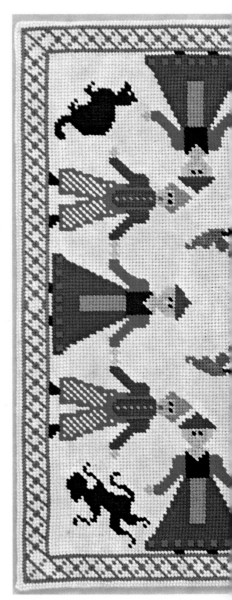

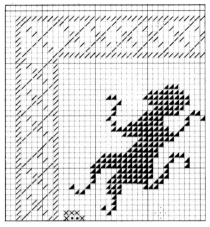

□ CREAM

◪ DARK BROWN

⊞ GOLDEN ORANGE

◪ BRIGHT GREEN

⊡ RED

◼ BLACK

⊟ BRIGHT YELLOW

⊠ MEDIUM BLUE

⊡ PALE PINK

⊞ DEEP ROSE

NURSERY RHYME RUG

NATURE'S KINGDOM RUG

Nature's tranquil panorama is translated in quick point to make a handsome rug in lush jungle colors. The majestic lion in the foreground is pictured with twelve of his subjects.

SIZE: 30" x 59".

EQUIPMENT: Masking tape. Pencil. Ruler. Extra-large-eyed tapestry needle. Scissors. **For Blocking:** Soft wooden surface. Brown wrapping paper. Square. Rustproof thumbtacks.

MATERIALS: Rug canvas, 5 mesh to the inch, 40" wide, 1⅞ yds. Rug yarn: ½ lb. each of hunter green, dark olive green, celery green, gray-blue green, chartreuse green, bottle green, gold; ¼ lb. each of pale pink, shrimp pink, russet brown, dark greenish brown, dark brown, medium brown, gray-beige, purple, pale blue, medium blue, white.

DIRECTIONS: Read general directions on page 105. With pencil, mark outline of area to be worked, 30" x 59". Following chart, work picture in continental or diagonal stitch, using one strand of yarn in needle.

When rug is complete, block as directed and finish edges as desired; see page 106.

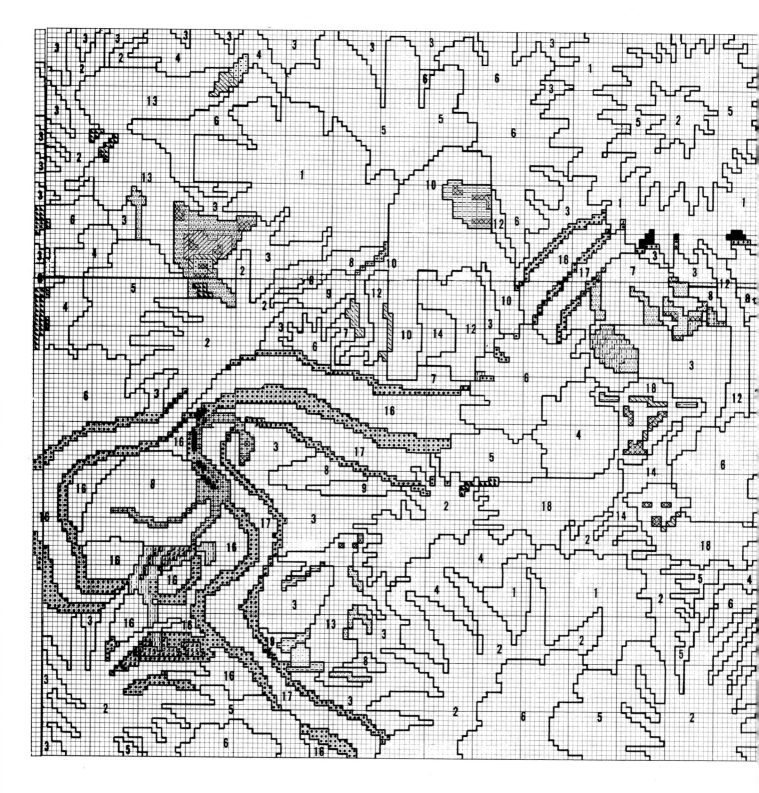

chart no.

	1	HUNTER GREEN		10	RUSSET BROWN
	2	DARK OLIVE GREEN	⊠	11	DARK GREENISH BROWN
◣	3	CELERY GREEN		12	DARK BROWN
	4	GRAY-BLUE GREEN		13	MEDIUM BROWN
	5	CHARTREUSE GREEN	◨	14	GRAY-BEIGE
	6	BOTTLE GREEN	◉	15	PURPLE
⊞	7	GOLD	⧄	16	PALE BLUE
⊟	8	PALE PINK	◼	17	MEDIUM BLUE
⊞	9	SHRIMP PINK	⊡	18	WHITE

130

COLOR SELECTION: Large areas of one color have been
blocked off and numbered according to the chart number
listed in color key. Smaller areas of these colors are desig-
nated by symbols as shown on the color key.

"PERUVIAN" RUG

Peruvian art inspired the stylized birds and interlocking fishes in this stunning design. Needle-point and latch-hook panels alternate.

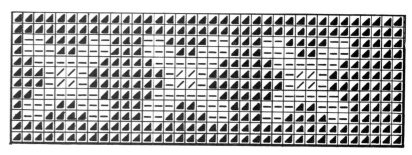

CHART A

SIZE: 41" x 70".

EQUIPMENT: Large-eyed rug needle. Latch (latchet) hook. Scissors. Large-eyed sewing needle.

MATERIALS: Rug yarn, 1-oz. skeins: red, 8 skeins; dark orange, 5 skeins; light orange, 7 skeins; dark olive green, 38 skeins; bronze green, 31 skeins. Rug canvas, 4 mesh to the inch, 42" wide, 2 yds. Rug binding, 7 yds. Carpet thread.

DIRECTIONS: Rug is worked in alternating tufted and flat bands. The tufted bands are worked with a latch hook; read general directions for latch hooking on page 39. Cut yarn into short strands as you need them, as instructed. The flat bands may be worked in either needlepoint or cross-stitch. Before beginning rug, work samples in both techniques with the yarn and canvas chosen and with the yarn both single and double in the needle, to determine which technique fits the canvas best. To work needlepoint, read general directions on page 105; to work cross-stitch, see details on page 136.

Place canvas on flat surface with selvages at sides. Rug is worked from top to bottom, starting with a latch-hook band. At top end, turn 1" of canvas to front and work latch-hook knots through double thickness of canvas, following latch-hook instructions. Following chart A, above, work twelve rows across with dark olive green background, bronze and light orange designs; there are five background stitches at beginning and end of each row (right end of chart is right-hand edge of canvas); repeat chart across, with three background stitches between each repeat.

Next band across is worked in needlepoint or cross-stitch. Following chart D for bird design, work band across, reversing direction of birds where indicated in illustration on page 133. If working in cross-stitch, be sure all bottom and top stitches of crosses are made in same direction throughout.

Next, work band of latch hooks across, following chart B and using bronze green for background and dark olive and red for design (right end of chart is right-hand edge of canvas).

Work next flat band, using chart C for fishes; repeat chart across.

Then make another latch-hook band, following chart A. Repeat bands, following illustration, to other end of canvas, marking eight flat bands and nine latch-hook bands. When working last latch-hook band, stop when four rows from end. Cut off canvas beyond eight rows; turn four rows of canvas over to front and work last four rows through double canvas.

Finish according to directions on page 106.

RED ☒

DARK ORANGE ·

LIGHT ORANGE ╱

DARK OLIVE GREEN ◢

BRONZE GREEN —

134

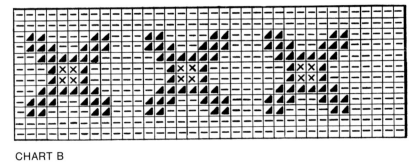

CHART B

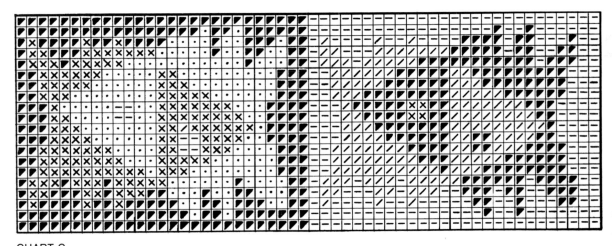

CHART C

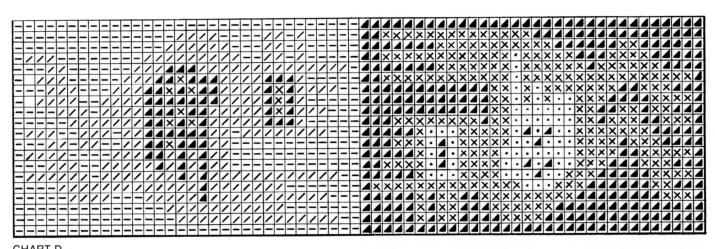

CHART D

DIAGONAL METHOD OF WORKING CROSS-STITCHES

CROSS-STITCH

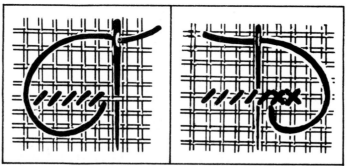

figure 1   figure 2

To work cross-stitch on canvas, bring needle to front at
left. Cross mesh diagonally, insert needle and bring out in
mesh below (Fig. 1). Continue across. To return and complete stitches, cross mesh diagonally in opposite direction,
insert needle and bring out in mesh below (Fig. 2).

6

Woven Rugs

Handloom weaving has been revived today with such enthusiasm and interest that it is truly one of this country's most popular and exciting crafts. The abundance of high-quality, colorful weaving yarn, the variety of looms for every level of skill, and the simplification of technical instruction combine to bring weaving into the range of anyone who is interested. On the following pages you will find two exceptionally beautiful weaving patterns that can be executed on both large and small looms.

NAVAJO MAT

An old Navajo mat fits in beautifully with contemporary decor. It can be woven on an authentic Navajo loom or conventional tapestry or 2-harness loom. For a rug, sew three mats together!

SIZE: 18″ x 37″.

EQUIPMENT: Tapestry or 2-harness loom. Beater (such as a table fork). Shuttles or bobbins. Paper for pattern. Ruler. Pencil. Scissors.

MATERIALS: For warp: Rug warp, 8/4, 220 yds. For weft: Medium-weight, single-ply wool yarn of uniform size (sometimes called "fine" yarn by handspun yarn suppliers): white (or natural), orange, mixed brown-black, mixed brown-white, mixed orange-brown, 4 ozs. each; red, 1 oz. Scrap yarn. White, 2-ply heavy yarn for edgings, about 9 yds. (**Note:** This is an old piece that combines natural-color yarns with yarns colored with commercial dyes; it would be difficult to duplicate the colors exactly. For example, the orange-brown yarn was probably obtained by spinning brown fleece with white fleece into a brown-white yarn, then dipping the yarn into an orange commercial dye. You can, however, obtain similar interesting effects with many modern yarns, both handspun and commercial.)

DIRECTIONS: Warp loom according to manufacturer's directions. Make warp about 55″ long (length of weaving plus 18″ for tying up and warp lost). There are 144 warp ends. For a 2-harness loom, thread in a straight draw (1,2), one end per heddle. Draw ends through an 8-dent reel, one end per dent. Width of warp is 18″.

For cartoon, enlarge pattern by copying on paper ruled in 2″ squares; complete quarter-pattern indicated by dash lines. Darken the outlines so they are visible when placed under warp. Weave about 1″ heading, using scrap yarn; this will be removed later. Place cartoon below warp, and pin bottom edge to heading. If desired, transfer the outlines to warp threads with waterproof ink. (**Note:** It may be necessary to cut up the cartoon into sections to fit behind warp when using a 2-harness loom.) Wind shuttles or bobbins of each color and follow color key for placement of colors.

Weaving: Cut two pieces of white 2-ply heavy yarn, each 2 yds. long, for edging. Tie ends together around left side of loom frame above heading, wrapping around frame several times. Twine pieces together with fingers (see "Twining" detail opposite) through warp; wrap ends around right frame of loom and tie securely. (If working on a harness loom, edging may have to be untied from sides of loom before completing piece; tie loose ends into a knot at each corner and let ends dangle.) Selvage cords also may be woven into each side of mat as illustrated. (These cords were used to add strength to Navajo rugs and saddle blankets and may be omitted if desired.) Cut two long strands of heavy 2-ply white yarn, each about 2½ yds. long. Wrap one strand around bottom of loom frame at left of warp, wrapping center of strand twice around frame; bring ends up to top of loom frame, wrap around twice, and tie. One half of cord will lie directly above other half. Repeat at right of warp with second long strand. Tension of selvage is snug but not as tight as warp. As you work, weave around top half of each cord, going around cord and outer warp end as if they were one end. Leave bottom half of cord free. After twelve rows (six weft turns on each side), untie each cord at top of loom, twist so that bottom half is now on top, and retie. Continue as before, untying, twisting, and retying after every twelve rows.

Mat is woven in plain weave. Weave the first stripe, beating down hard to cover the warp completely. Throw a shot of white, then weave the second stripe. To weave pattern, work all areas across simultaneously, using several bobbins of the same color where necessary; do not carry a color from one area over to another. Open shed; throw one shot of each required color within the outlined areas only. Beat down. Leave bobbins hanging in place. Change shed, and throw the next shot of each color in the opposite direction. Continue weaving back and forth within the outlined areas. Where colors meet on a diagonal, they lie next to each other between warp ends (see "Straight Edge" detail). Where colors meet to form a vertical line, they are "teethed," i.e., they lie next to each other between alternating warp ends (see "Serrated Edge" detail). Weave in ends as you go. (The Navajo method: Yarn is broken rather than cut, to leave tapered ends; to break, untwist against the spin and pull. Broken ends of one color are overlapped 1″ in same shed; new colors are brought just to pattern line; the heavy beat holds ends in place.)

Finishing: When weaving is completed, twine an edging cord as at beginning, using either the 2-ply white heavy yarn as before or the orange yarn, as illustrated. Untie selvage cords and edging cords from the loom and tie them together at corners. Remove heading. Knot warp ends close to weaving and trim close.

Rug: To make a rug 3 ft. x 4½ ft., make three mats as above, omitting the selvage cords from one mat and from one side of the other two mats. Sides of the three mats must be kept straight. Sew mats together as shown in diagram, tying the edging cords of adjacent mats together where they meet.

QUARTER-PATTERN FOR MAT

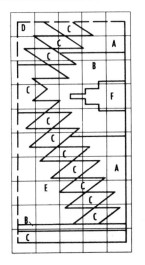

A   WHITE OR NATURAL
B   ORANGE
C   BROWN-BLACK
D   BROWN-WHITE
E   ORANGE-BROWN
F   RED

SERRATED EDGE

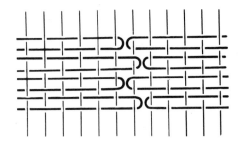

STRAIGHT EDGE

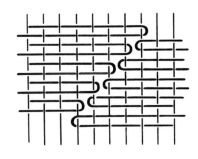

THREE MATS MAKE RUG

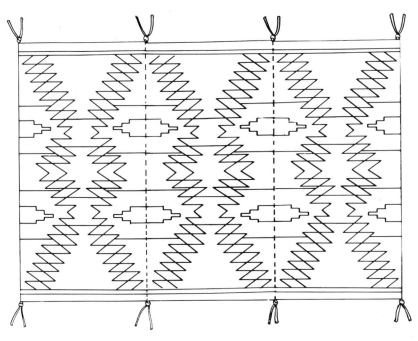

TWINING

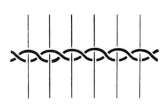

HARVEST SUN RUG

A half sun sinks into reflecting bands of color to reappear on the other side. Each rib-weave band merges into the next by changing one color.

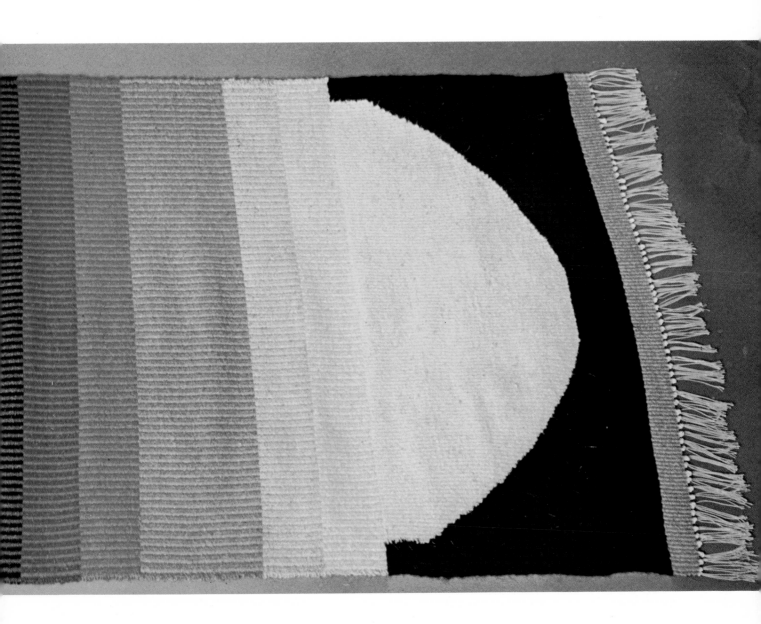

SIZE: 27″ x 74″ (plus fringe).

EQUIPMENT: Four-harness loom with weaving width of 27″. Beater. Shuttles. Scissors. Ruler. Pencil. Paper for pattern.

MATERIALS: For warp: 3-ply cotton warp, about 720 yds. For weft: single-ply heavy cow's-hair yarn put up in 110-yd., 4-oz. skeins: 5 skeins each yellow and dark brown, 3 skeins each yellow-orange and orange, 2 skeins each yellow-gold, bright orange, and medium brown. Rug linen, 1 oz.

DIRECTIONS: Warp loom according to manufacturer's directions. Warp is 96″ long (length of rug plus 24″ for tie-up and warp lost). There are 270 warp ends; draw them in a 10-dent reed, one end per dent. (See "Threading" and "Tie-up" drafts on the following page.)

Enlarge half-pattern for sun shape by copying on paper ruled in 1″ squares; complete half-pattern indicated by dash lines. Darken outline so it is visible when placed behind warp. When indicated, place pattern under warp and trace outline onto warp. Use yellow for sun, and wind an extra shuttle of dark brown for background. Follow weaving draft, using both colors. To avoid a slit in straight areas of sun shape, interlock adjacent wefts every few shots, as shown in diagram. The remainder of the weaving consists of horizontal stripes with interlocking vertical stripes. For each horizontal stripe, use two shuttles, one of each color indicated; throw one shot of first color, change shed, and throw a shot of second color. When changing colors for the next horizontal stripe, make sure that the color carried over from the previous stripe is woven in the same shed as before. Thus a continuous vertical stripe of the color is formed through all the adjacent horizontal stripes in which it appears.

Weaving: Follow draft for weaving and beat tightly, so no warp shows. Weave 3″ heading with heavy scrap yarn.

   *1″ linen
   4¾″ dark brown (then trace sun outline on warp)
   11½″ yellow for sun area, with brown background
   3″ yellow/yellow-gold
   3″ yellow-gold/yellow-orange
   6″ yellow-orange/orange
   3″ orange/bright orange
   3″ bright orange/medium brown*
   6″ medium brown/dark brown

Repeat from * to * in reverse, to make symmetrical design.

Finishing: Remove weaving from loom; remove heading. Separate warp ends into groups of four. With each group, tie a single knot close to weaving. Trim ends to 3″.

HALF-PATTERN FOR SUN

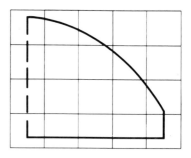

STRAIGHT LINES OF SUN

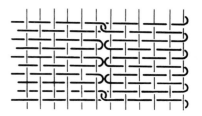

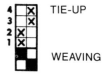

TIE-UP

WEAVING

THREADING

7

Rya and Flossa Rugs

The rya or flossa knotted rug is characterized by brilliant and vibrant coloring. The effect is achieved by the special way in which closely related colors are used together, either by combining several shades in the same knot or by placing almost identical shades side by side. Usually the rug has a simple and unified theme, expressed by its design as well as the blending of color.

The modern rya and flossa rugs, with their rich and subtle color shading and abstract patterns, are an exciting design element in contemporary settings. Yet the technique for making the knot used in these rugs is an old one. In fact, the oldest existing carpet, found in Central Asia and dating from 500 B.C., is made with the same knot, known as the Turkey, or Ghiordes, knot. This rug shows a high degree of skill, indicating a development over many previous centuries.

Perhaps the Vikings learned the technique from the Persians, whose merchant ships they plundered. Another theory says that slaves the Vikings brought from Ireland might have introduced ryas and flossas into Scandinavia.

The first coarse rugs the Vikings wove were really clothing, to protect themselves in their open sailing vessels. The early Scandinavians made rugs in imitation of sheep- and bearskins, to use in sleighs or to warm an alcove. Later, rugs were hung on the wall to keep out drafts, and finally they became coverings for the floor.

The terms "flossa" and "rya" are sometimes used interchangeably. There is, however, a subtle difference between the two, although both rugs are made with the Ghiordes knot. In the flossa the knotted rows are made closer together, producing a firm, thick, upright pile that gives a deep, velvety surface. In the rya (the word means "rough" or "rough hair" in Swedish) the tufted rows are farther apart, with more tabby weaving (plain weaving) between the rows. Thus tufts lie flatter, with variable and shaggy texture.

True rya and flossa rugs are woven on a handloom, and the knotted fringe is made at the same time. These rugs have become so popular in recent years, however, that a special foundation fabric is now available for the nonweaver that is woven with openwork rows at even intervals, into which the flossa or rya knots can be made.

general directions

When working a flossa or rya rug on a fabric background, the same Ghiordes knot is used to make the fringe as for the handwoven rug, but it is worked with a needle through the openwork rows instead of on a loom. The finished effect is the same as that of a handwoven flossa or rya rug.

The pattern is often indicated on a chart with a color key. The rows of knots are made with a large-eyed needle, threaded with from two to six strands of lightweight rug yarn or tapestry yarn, usually in related colors. Use as many needles as there are combinations of colors in the rug. The knots may be made over a ruler or similar gauge as wide as the rug's pile is long, but some prefer to work without a gauge. Rug piles vary from about ¾" to 2¾". It is not essential that the knots be absolutely the same length; in fact, they should vary slightly, to avoid ridges in the finished rug.

Usually the knots are worked from selvage to selvage of the foundation. However, if you cut the fabric to make a smaller width, machine-stitch first at the turnover point, cut fabric ½" beyond stitching, turn under, and stitch twice to the foundation fabric.

When the knotting is completed, the two ends of the foundation must be finished. Ravel each end of foundation for 3" to 4", ending at an openwork row and leaving a fringe of warp threads. Knot and weave in fringe as shown in "Edge Finish" (see below). A rug may also be finished with a twisted fringe; see "Bull's-Eye Rug" on opposite page.

Rya or Flossa Knot

Knots are worked only in the openwork rows of foundation fabric. Work each row across from left to right, starting at bottom of foundation fabric and working up. Each stitch is worked over two groups of threads. Starting at left edge, skip first space, insert needle under the next group of threads, right to left (Fig. 1). Pull yarn through, leaving an end the length of intended pile. Holding this end below row with left thumb, insert needle under next group of threads, from right to left (Fig. 2); pull tight to make first knot stitch.

Holding yarn below row with left thumb, insert needle under next group of threads, from right to left (Fig. 3). Pull yarn up, leaving loop of desired length below row. Continue across row to right edge, working Figs. 2 and 3 and making each loop approximately the same length. Leave the last space in a row unworked.

If desired, use a ruler or other gauge after making the first stitch, to make loops uniform, bringing yarn under ruler to begin each new stitch (Fig. 4); do not pull yarn too tightly around ruler. Push ruler to right as work proceeds and pull out at end of row.

Cut each row of loops with scissors as it is completed, to insure that all loops are cut. When changing colors, work across row to the color change and cut yarn to length of loop after completing last knot of first color. Start new color as in Fig. 1 under next group of threads. Work across row in pattern before starting next row up.

Edge Finish

With wrong side of rug up, knot strands together in bunches of three. Push knots up to edge of foundation fabric and tighten (Fig. 1).

Take third bunch of knotted strands, bring under second, over first, around and under first, over second, and under fourth; bring up over fabric and pin to hold (Fig. 2).

Take first bunch of knotted strands, bring under second, over third, and under fourth; bring up over foundation, being careful not to pull yarn tight; pin. Continue in this manner (Fig. 3) until all strands are plaited.

With crochet hook, weave ends of bunches in and out of foundation and clip off the excess thread ends.

RYA KNOT

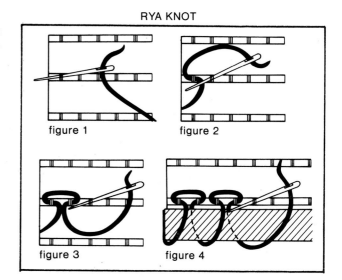

figure 1   figure 2

figure 3   figure 4

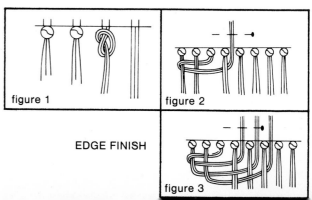

figure 1   figure 2

EDGE FINISH

figure 3

BULL'S-EYE RUG

A rya bull's-eye over stripes gives a dramatic "rug-on-rug" effect. This handsome design makes a stunning wall hanging too.

SIZE: 39" x 51" unfringed.

EQUIPMENT: Ruler. Pencil, string, and large straight pin to make compass. Rug needles with very large eyes. Scissors.

MATERIALS: Woven rya backing, 39" wide, 59" long (this allows for fringe at each end); without fringe, backing required is 39" x 51". Rug yarn, 3½ oz. 130-yd. skeins: wine, 11½ skeins; dark purple, 3½ skeins; dark orange, 6½ skeins; light orange, 2 skeins; brown, 6½ skeins; pale yellow, 7½ skeins.

DIRECTIONS: Read general directions on opposite page. Make compass by tying long length of string to pencil; make knot on string at point 19" from pencil. Lay rya backing out flat. With pin, secure outer knot of string to exact center of backing; hold in place with fingers of one hand. With other hand, hold pencil in upright position; swing pencil around to mark 38" diameter circle on backing. Make four more concentric circles within this circle, adjusting space between pencil and outer knot as follows: 13", 9", 5½", 2¾", making 26", 18", 11", and 5½" diameter circles. Go over circles with heavy pencil or waterproof ink marker if necessary.

To work rya, thread needle with three strands of yarn and make rya knots in the openwork rows of holes in the backing. If making fringed rug, start at eleventh row of holes from bottom end and stop at eleventh row from other end, to allow for fringe. Leave first two and last two spaces in each row unworked. Make pile about 1¾" long.

Work rug in rows of colors as follows: Two rows of pale yellow, two brown, two pale yellow, two brown, two pale yellow. From this point on, work circle area while continuing to work background stripes, completing each row across. Use wine for outer circle,

dark orange for next circle, dark purple for the next, light orange for the next, and dark orange for center circle. Continue alternating two rows each of brown and pale yellow at each end of row outside circle.

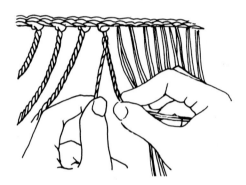

TWISTED FRINGE

Twisted Fringe: When knotting is complete, cut weft (horizontal) threads at each side end and between warp (vertical) threads where necessary up to ninth row of backing; pull away weft, leaving only warp threads. Warp is arranged in groups of three threads each. With first group of three threads make knot and push knot up to edge of backing; pull tight. Repeat with second group of three threads. Twist first and second groups simultaneously to the left, using thumb and index finger of each hand; keep twisting until tight. While twisting, lay the first group over the second and twist to the right until both groups are tightly twisted together; knot together at bottom end. See detail above. Repeat with each two groups across each end of rug.

BULL'S-EYE RUG

REFLECTED SHADOWS RUG

This classic rya pattern with its subtle blend of colors and harmonious theme gives an impressionistic feeling of trees and shadows at the water's edge.

COMBINATION NO. 1 ⊠
COMBINATION NO. 2 ◉
COMBINATION NO. 3 ▨
COMBINATION NO. 4 ▦

SIZE: 20″ x 30″.

EQUIPMENT: Four rug needles with very large eyes. Needle with medium eye. Scissors.

MATERIALS: Tapestry yarn, 8-yd. skeins: deep purple, 12 skeins; purple, 24 skeins; light purple, 12 skeins; bright blue, 40 skeins; pale blue, 20 skeins; light blue, 10 skeins; medium blue, 20 skeins; dark blue, 10 skeins; medium-bright blue, 16 skeins; deep blue, 16 skeins; apple green, 32 skeins; medium yellow-green, 32 skeins; forest green, 32 skeins. Woven rya foundation fabric, 1 yd. White sewing thread.

DIRECTIONS: Read general directions on page 144. Cut off a strip along one selvage edge, making foundation fabric 22″ x 36″. Stitch cut edge as directed with white thread.

Six strands of yarn were used in needle to make the knots. Thread each of the four large-eyed needles with six strands in the following combinations of colors: No 1: one deep purple, two purple, one light purple, two bright blue; No. 2: two pale blue, one light blue, two medium blue, one dark blue; No. 3: two apple green, two medium yellow-green, two forest green; No. 4: two medium-bright blue, two bright blue, two deep blue.

The No. 1 combination is represented on chart by the X symbol; No. 2 combination is a dot; No. 3 combination is a diagonal slash line; No. 4 combination is a solid black square.

With selvage and stitched edges at sides, begin 3″ up from bottom edge. Work knots across open rows, following details on page 144. Each square of chart is a knot. Work the number of knots of one color combination indicated on chart, cut yarn; continue with each color combination across row. When knotting is complete, finish edges as indicated on page 144.

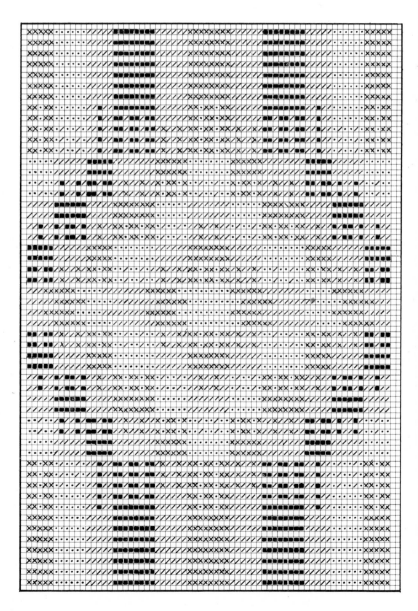

REFLECTED SHADOWS RUG

Knitted and Crocheted Rugs

Knitting and crochet cannot be overlooked for their adaptability in rugmaking. Naturally, experience with basic knitting and crochet techniques is recommended before attempting the projects that follow, but you need *only* the basics—the rug instructions are simple!

general directions

HOW TO KNIT

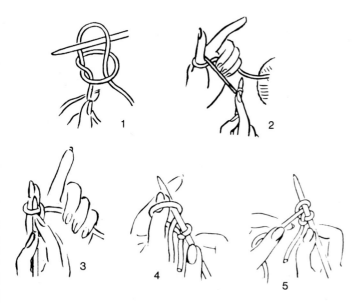

TO CAST ON: 1. Make a slip loop on needle. 2. Loop yarn around left thumb. 3. Insert needle. 4. Remove thumb. 5. Pull yarn to tighten stitch. Repeat Figs. 2-5 for desired number of stitches.

TO KNIT(k): 1. Hold needle with cast-on stitches in left hand. Weave yarn over index finger of right hand, under middle finger, over third finger and under little finger. Hold second needle in right hand like a pencil. With yarn in back of work, insert right needle in the front of first stitch toward back. 2. Put yarn around needle. 3. Pull loop of yarn through the stitch. 4. Slip stitch off left needle.

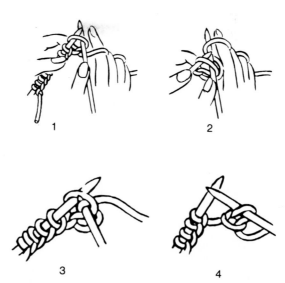

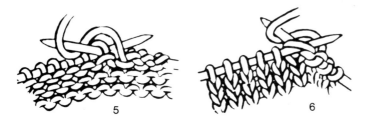

TO PURL (p): 5. With yarn in front of work, insert needle from right to left in first stitch, put yarn around needle, pull loop through stitch. Slip stitch off needle.

SEED STITCH: 6. Cast on an uneven number of stitches. * Knit 1, purl 1; repeat from * across; end with knit 1. Repeat this row for seed-stitch pattern.

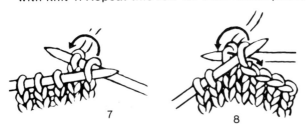

TO BIND OFF (7 and 8): Knit 2 stitches. * With left needle, bring first stitch on right needle over second stitch and off needle. Knit next stitch and repeat from *

Yo When Knitting: Bring yarn under right-hand needle to front, then over needle to back, ready to knit next stitch.

Yo When Purling: Wind yarn around right-hand needle once. Yarn is in position to purl next stitch.

Pick Up and Knit Stitches on Edge: From right side, insert needle into edge of work, put yarn around needle, finish as a k st. When picking up on bound-off or cast-on edge, pick up and k 1 st in each st (going through 2 lps at top of each bound-off or cast-on st); pick up and k l st in each knot formed on edge of each row on front or side edges.

To Slip a Stitch: Insert needle in st as if to knit st (unless directions read "as if to p") and sl st from one needle to the other without knitting or purling it.

Psso (pass slip stitch over): This is a decrease stitch. When directions read "sl 1, k 1, psso," insert left-hand needle from left to right under slipped stitch on right-hand needle, bring it over the knit stitch and off needle.

Garter St: K every row.

Stockinette St: K 1 row, p l row. When knitting round and round on circular or dp needles, k every row.

Seed St: With odd number of sts, k 1, p 1 across, ending k 1. Repeat row, having k 1 over a p st and p 1 over a k st.

* (asterisk): Repeat from directions following * as many extra times as directed. " * 2 dc in next st, 1 dc in next st, repeat from * 4 times" means to work directions after first * until second * is reached, then go back to first * 4 times more. Work 5 times in all.

( ) (parentheses): When parentheses are used to show repetition, work directions in parentheses as many times as specified. " (Dc, ch 1) 3 times" means to do what is in ( ) 3 times altogether.

† (dagger): Used same way as * when another symbol is needed.

Multiple: In pattern stitches, multiple means number of sts required for 1 pattern. Number of sts on needle should be evenly divisible by the multiple. If pattern is a multiple of 6 sts, number of sts to be worked might be 180, 186, 192, etc. If directions say "multiple of 6 sts plus 2," 2 extra sts are required: 182, 188, 194, etc.

Work even: Work in same stitch without increasing or decreasing.

HOW TO CROCHET

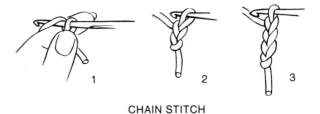

CHAIN STITCH

CHAIN STITCH (ch st): Make loop on hook. 1. Pass hook under yarn to catch yarn with hook. 2. Draw yarn through first loop. 3. Repeat to make required number of chains.

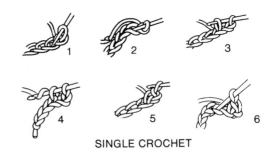

SINGLE CROCHET

SINGLE CROCHET (sc): 1. Insert hook under top 2 threads of 2nd chain from hook. 2. Catch yarn with hook. 3. Draw through chain. 4. Yarn over hook. 5. Draw yarn through 2 loops on hook—1 sc made. 6. Insert hook in next chain and repeat. At end of row, chain 1, turn work so reverse side is facing you. Work first single crochet of next row under top 2 threads of first stitch.

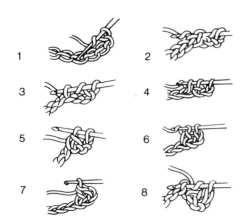

DOUBLE CROCHET

hook—1 dc made. 8. Yarn over hook, insert hook in next chain and repeat from 2. At end of row, chain 3 to turn. Turn work so reverse side is facing you. Turning chain is counted as first double crochet of next row. Work 2nd double crochet under top 2 threads of next double crochet of first row.

Half Double Crochet: Start with a loop on hook, put yarn over hook, insert hook in work, draw yarn through, yarn over hook and draw through all three loops on hook.

Treble Crochet: This is made the same way as double crochet, with the yarn wrapped around the hook twice instead of once and then worked off—yarn over and through two loops, yarn over and through two loops, yarn over and through two loops. For a **Double Treble**, yarn over the hook three times; and for a **Triple Treble**, yarn over the hook four times, taking off two loops at a time as in the treble crochet.

Picot: To make a picot, ch 3, 4, or required number, sc or sl st in first st of ch.

Slip Stitch: Insert hook through st, catch yarn, and, with one motion, draw through both the st and the one lp on hook. The sl st is used for joining.

DOUBLE CROCHET (dc): 1. Yarn over hook, insert hook under top 2 threads of 4th chain from hook. 2. Catch yarn with hook. 3. Draw yarn through chain. 4. Yarn over hook. 5. Draw through 2 loops on hook. 6. Yarn over hook. 7. Draw through remaining 2 loops on

ABBREVIATIONS AND STITCHES

Knitting Needles															
U.S.	0	1	2	3	4	5	6	7	8	9	10	10½	11	13	15
ENGLISH	13	12	11	10	9	8	7	6	5	4	3	2	1	00	000
CONTINENTAL — MM.	2¼	2½	3	3¼	3½	4	4½	5	5½	6	6½	7	7½	8½	9

Crochet Hooks (Aluminum or Plastic)										
U.S.	1/B	2/C	3/D	4/E	5/F	6/G	8/H	9/I	10/J	10½/K
ENGLISH	12	11	10	9	8	7	6	5	4	2
CONTINENTAL — MM.	2½	3		3½	4	4½	5	5½	6	7

KNITTING: Abbreviations, Stitches

k—knit
st (s)—stitch (es)
yo—yarn over
sl—slip
inc—increase
tog—together
dp—double-pointed
psso—pass slip stitch over
beg—beginning

MC—main color
CC—contrasting color
p—purl
rnd—round
sk—skip
pat—pattern
dec—decrease
lp—loop

CROCHET: Abbreviations, Stitches

beg—beginning
ch—chain
sl st—slip stitch
sc—single crochet
dc—double crochet
st (s)—stitch (es)
tr—treble crochet
dtr—double treble
tr tr—triple treble
hdc—half double crochet

rnd—round
p—picot
sp—space
bl—block
sk—skip
lp—loop
inc—increase
dec—decrease
yo—yarn over

YELLOW ROSE RUG

A single yellow rose blooms on a white pile rug to create a dramatic focal point and fresh new accent for a bedroom setting. Fringe is knotted into a knitted base with a large-eyed needle.

1

2

3

WHITE ☐
LIGHT YELLOW ☐•
ORANGE ☒

SIZE: About 40″ x 60″.

MATERIALS: Rayon-and-cotton rug yarn, 70-yd. skeins: 55 white, 3 orange, 2 light yellow. No. 10 knitting needle: 14″, jumper, or circular (or English size 3). Aluminum crochet hook size G. Three large-eyed yarn needles.

GAUGE: 3 sts = 1″; 7 rows = 1″.

DIRECTIONS: Foundation: With white, cast on 120 sts. **Row 1:** Knit.

Row 2: Purl.

Rows 3-5: Knit. Repeat rows 2-5 for pattern until there are 100 ridges (formed by row 4 of the pattern). Work row 5 of the last repeat. Purl 1 row. Bind off in knitting on next row.

Edging: With white and crochet hook, work 1 row sc around rug, working 1 sc in each st at ends of rug, 1 sc in every other row at sides of rug, and 3 sc in each corner. Join, cut yarn. Weave in ends.

Fringe: Thread a 6-yd. length of white in yarn needle. Bring ends together to form a double strand. Working from left to right in first ridge row, draw yarn up through first st, leaving 1¼″ ends.

Insert needle up through same st and to the right of hanging ends, pull yarn through until there is a small loop, draw yarn from right to left through small loop; tighten knot.

* Insert needle from bottom up through ridge of next st (Fig. 1). Pull yarn through, holding 1¼″ loop under thumb.

Insert needle to right of loop up through same st (Fig. 2). Pull yarn through, leaving a loop.

Put needle through this loop (Fig. 3). Tighten knot. Repeat from * across row.

Cut through loops. Loops may be cut after each row or after entire rug is completed.

Work 5 rows of white fringe at bottom of rug. On 6th ridge row (first row at bottom of chart, at left), work 79 loops of white, skip 1 st, finish row with 40 loops of white. In skipped st, knot orange, leaving ends as for beginning of row. Cut off orange 1¼″ from knot.

Continue to work from chart, making loops in every st of every ridge row. Each square across chart equals 1 st. Every other row of squares on chart represents one ridge row of rug. There are 20 loops of white to left of chart and 15 loops of white to right of chart which are not shown.

When top of chart is reached, work remaining ridge rows in white, to finish the rug.

NORTHERN LIGHTS RUG

A luxurious shag rug repeats the brilliant hues of northern lights. The technique is easy: a filet-mesh backing is crocheted in a solid color, then yarn strands are knotted through.

SIZE: 48″ x 78″

MATERIALS: Heavy rayon-cotton rug yarn, 70-yd. skeins: For crocheted mesh background, 24 skeins turquoise. For fringed surface, 26 skeins royal blue, 17 skeins emerald, 10 skeins turquoise, 4 skeins navy, 3 skeins each dark orange, red, and dark red. Aluminum crochet hook size J.

GAUGE: 3 sts = 1″ (before fringing).

Note: After fringing, crocheted background becomes narrower and longer.

CROCHETED MESH BACKGROUND: With turquoise, ch 168.

Row 1: Sc in 2nd ch from hook and in each ch across—167 sc. Ch 1 to turn each row.

Row 2: Sc in first sc, * ch 1, sk 1 sc, sc in next sc, repeat from * across—84 sc.

Row 3: Sc in first sc, * ch 1, sc in next sc, repeat from * across—84 sc. Repeat row 3 until there are 143 mesh rows.

Next Row: Sc in each sc and ch-1 sp across. End off.

FRINGED PATTERN: Open up skein of rug yarn. Cut through all strands at both ends of skein; strands are about 24″ long. Cut all strands into 6″ lengths.

To fringe, hold two strands together, fold strands in half. Insert hook down and up under 1 sc, catch folded loop of strands and draw under sc; draw 4 ends through loop; tighten knot.

Beginning with first mesh row, knot a fringe around every sc, including first and last sc of each row. Follow chart on page 156 for colors of fringe. Each square on chart represents one fringe. Note that some color symbols represent two colors. Knot these fringes with one strand of each color.

When top of chart has been reached, turn chart upside down. Work rows 49 to 1.

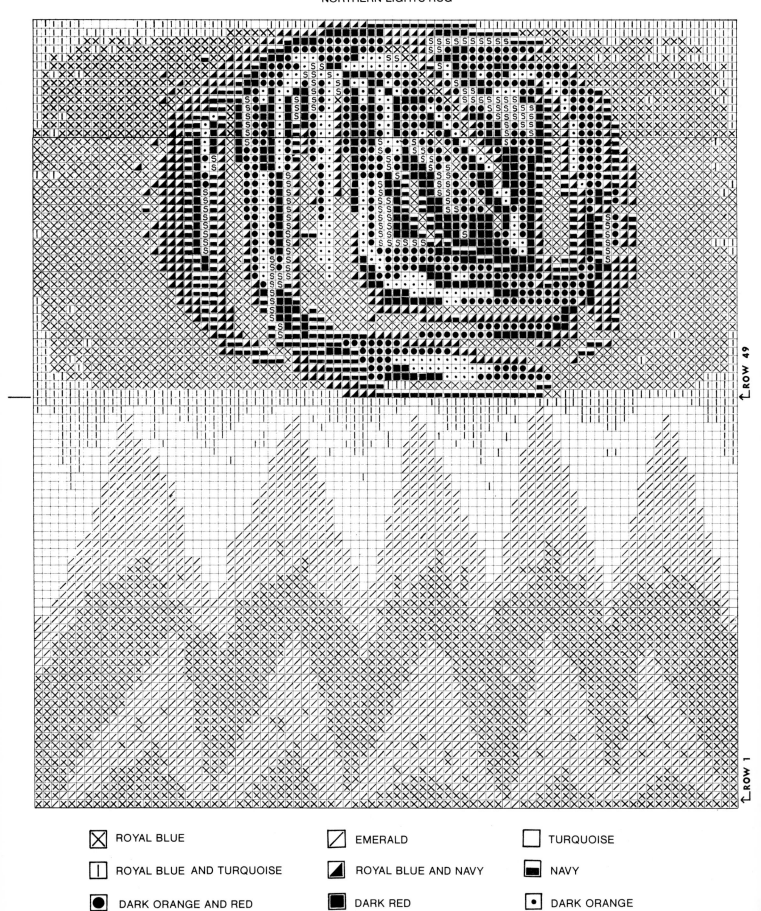

ROW 49

ROW 1

	ROYAL BLUE		EMERALD		TURQUOISE
	ROYAL BLUE AND TURQUOISE		ROYAL BLUE AND NAVY		NAVY
	DARK ORANGE AND RED		DARK RED		DARK ORANGE
	RED AND DARK RED				

156

CABLE-CORD CROCHETED RUG

This oval rug combines two interesting crochet techniques: royal blue and turquoise rug yarn is crocheted over cable cord, and white fringe is knotted through filet mesh.

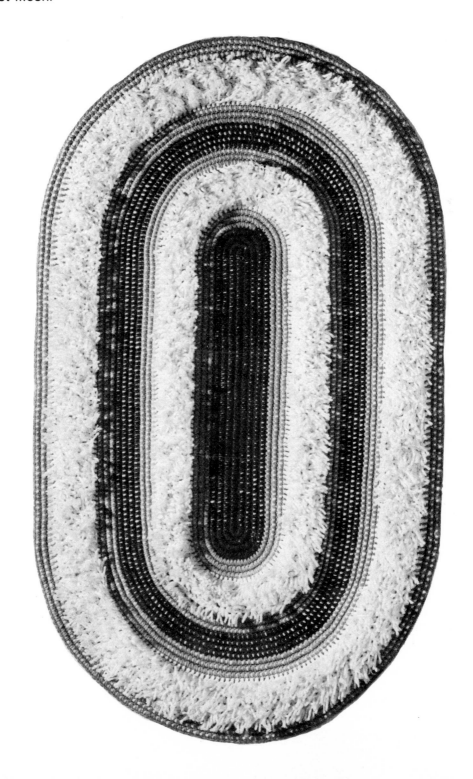

SIZE: 58″ x 33″.

MATERIALS: Rayon-and-cotton rug yarn, 70-yd. skeins: 14 white (W), 3 royal blue (B), 6 turquoise (T). Crochet hook size H. Cable cord, size 200, one 72-yd. spool.

DIRECTIONS: Notes: All B and T rnds are worked over cable cord. All W rnds are worked without cable cord. When working over cord, pull cord occasionally to straighten work.

Beg at center with B, ch 65 loosely to measure about 24″. **Rnd 1:** Lay end of cord behind lp on hook and over working strand. Working over cord, make 3 sc in 2nd ch from hook, sc in each of 62 ch, 5 sc in last ch; working back on other side of ch, sc in each of 62 ch. Working over starting end of cord and cord, 2 sc in same ch as first 3 sc. Cut off starting end of cord close to sts.

Mark last st of each rnd.

Rnd 2: Working over cord, 2 sc in each of 3 sc, sc in each of 62 sc, 2 sc in each of 5 sc, sc in each of 62 sc, 2 sc in each of 2 sc.

Rnd 3: 2 sc in each of next 5 sc, sc in each of 64 sc, 2 sc in each of next 8 sc, sc in each of 64 sc, 2 sc in each of last 3 sc.

Rnd 4: (Sc in next sc, 2 sc in next sc) 4 times, sc in 69 sc, (2 sc in next sc, sc in next sc) 5 times, 2 sc in next sc, sc in 69 sc, 2 sc in next sc, sc in next sc, 2 sc in last sc. Cut off cord close to last st. Sl st in first sc (not over cord). Cut B; pull end through lp on hook. Tighten lp.

Rnd 5: With T, make lp on hook. Working over cord and B end, sc in same sc as sl st. Sc in each sc around—172 sc.

Rnd 6: (2 sc in next sc, sc in next 2 sc) twice, 2 sc in next sc, sc in 76 sc, (2 sc in next sc, sc in next 2 sc) 3 times, 2 sc in next sc, sc in next 76 sc, 2 sc in next sc, sc in last sc.

Rnd 7: Sc in each sc—180 sc. Cut off cord close to last st. Sl st in first sc (not over cord). Cut T; pull end through lp on hook. Weave in end on wrong side.

Rnd 8: Attach W in first sc, ch 3 (to count as 1 dc), dc in next 4 sc, (2 dc in next sc, 1 dc in next 5 dc) 3 times, dec 1 st in next 2 sts (**to dec,*** yo hook, insert hook in next st, pull yarn through, yo and pull through 2 lps, repeat from * once, yo and pull through all 3 lps), dc in next 5 sts, (dec 1 st over next 2 sts, dc in next 5 sts) 7 times, dec over next 2 sts, dc in 2 sts, (2 dc in next sc, dc in 5 sc) 5 times, (dec 1 st over next 2 sts, dc in next 5 sc) 8 times, dec 1 st over next 2 sts, dc in next 2 sc, 2 dc in next st, dc in 5 sc, 2 dc in last sc, join in top of ch 3—172 dc.

Rnd 9: Sl st between first 2 dc, ch 4. **Note:** Work all dc rnds in sps between dc's. (Dc in next sp, ch 1) 18 times, dc in next 59 sps, (ch 1, dc in next sp) 27 times, dc in next 59 sps, (ch 1, dc in next sp) 8 times, ch 1, sl st in 3rd ch of ch 4—172 dc.

Rnd 10: Sl st in next sp, ch 4, dc in next sp, (ch 1, dc in next sp) 15 times, dc in next 63 sps, (ch 1, dc in next sp) 23 times, dc in next 63 sps, (ch 1, dc in next sp) 6 times, ch 1, sl st in 3rd ch of ch 4—172 dc.

Rnd 11: Sl st in next sp, ch 4, dc in next sp, (ch 1, dc in next sp) 15 times, dc in next 61 sps, (ch 1, dc in next sp) 25 times, dc in next 61 sps, (ch 1, dc in next sp) 8 times, ch 1, sl st in 3rd ch of ch 4—172 dc.

Rnd 12: Sl st in next sp, ch 4, (dc in next sp, ch 1) 4 times, dc in same sp as last dc, * (ch 1, dc in next sp) 5 times, ch 1, dc in same sp as last dc, repeat from * once, ch 1, dc in next sp, ch 1, dc in next 3 sps, 2 dc in next sp, (dc in next 6 sps, 2 dc in next sp) 8 times, dc in next 2 sps, (ch 1, dc in next sp) 3 times, ch 1, dc in same sp as last dc, * (ch 1, dc in next sp) 5 times, ch 1, dc in same sp as last dc, repeat from * 3 times, (ch 1, dc in next sp) twice, dc in next 3 sps, 2 dc in next sp, (dc in next 6 sps, 2 dc in next sp) 8 times, (dc in next sp, ch 1) 4 times, dc in same sp as last dc, (ch 1, dc in next sp) 5 times, ch 1, dc in same (last) sp, ch 1, sl st in 3rd ch of ch 4—200 dc. Cut off W.

Rnd 13: Attach T and cord. On curved ends, work 1 sc in each dc and in each ch-1 sp. On straight sides, work 1 sc in each sp between dc's.

Rnd 14: Sc in each sc.

Rnd 15: Sc in each sc. Join; cut T.

Rnd 16 and 17: Attach B, work even in sc.

Rnd 18: Working in sc, inc 8 sts evenly spaced around each curved end.

Rnd 19: Work even in sc. Join; cut B.

Rnd 20: Attach T; working in sc, inc 10 sts evenly spaced around each curved end.

Rnd 21: Work even in sc.

Rnd 22: Sc in each sc. Cut T and cord.

Rnd 23: Attach W, ch 3 for first dc, work dc in each sc around, dec 9 sts evenly spaced on each straight side. Join.

Rnd 24: Sl st in next sp, ch 3, 1 dc in each sp around. Join.

Rnd 25: Dc in each sp, inc 7 sts evenly spaced on each curved end. Join.

Rnd 26 and 27: Dc in each sp around. Join each rnd.

Rnd 28: Dc in each sp, inc 9 sts evenly spaced on each curved end. Cut W.

Rnd 29: Attach T and cord, sc in each sp around.

Rnd 30: Sc in each sc.

Rnd 31: Work in sc, inc 9 sts evenly spaced on each curved end. Join; cut T and cord.

FINISHING: Steam rug flat. For fringe, cut W into 4″ lengths. Knot over each dc of W rows as follows: fold strand in half, insert hook under dc, pull loop under dc, pick up ends and pull ends through loop. Tighten knot. Fringe all white areas of rug.

Appliquéd Rugs

Anyone who enjoys appliqué piecework will find that the rug shown on the following pages will inspire endless ideas for rugmaking projects using favorite appliqué motifs.

"HAWAIIAN" RUG

An allover pattern of leaves and curving branches is reminiscent of the giant appliqués of Hawaiian quilts. Here the design is machine-stitched through two layers; excess fabric is snipped away from one layer, leaving the appliqué.

SIZE: 64″ square.

EQUIPMENT: Paper for pattern. Pencil. Ruler. Yardstick. Tracing nylon 36″ wide, 1¾ yds. Straight pins. Sewing machine with zigzag attachment. Sewing needle. Regular and embroidery scissors.

MATERIALS: Felt, 72″ wide: 3¾ yards of moss green, two yards baby blue. Baby-blue and moss-green sewing thread.

DIRECTIONS: Enlarge pattern for one-quarter of the design by copying on paper ruled in 2″ squares. Place the quarter-pattern on flat surface and cover with tracing nylon; with pencil, go over pattern lines to mark design on nylon. Piece tracing nylon together with tape to make it large enough for entire design. Matching dash lines and retracing design three more times, complete entire design, including border, on nylon by moving pattern. Make sure center leaf motifs are all going in a clockwise direction.

From the green felt cut a piece 66″ square. Baste tracing nylon, with design centered, to green felt. From the blue felt cut a piece 65″ square; pin and baste blue felt to green felt on surface opposite tracing nylon; baste together along edges and across diagonally to secure. On sewing machine, using blue thread and zigzag attachment on #2 setting for tiny stitches, stitch, nylon side up, along all lines of design. Turn blue surface up, and, with embroidery scissors, cut away blue felt around all stitched motifs and border just outside stitching. Trim away nylon from wrong side.

From remaining green felt cut a piece the same size as rug for backing. Pin rug and backing together with right sides facing. With green thread, stitch together all around ½″ from cut edge; leave about 30″ open in center of one side. Turn rug to right side. Turn edges of opening in ½″ and slip-stitch closed.

10

Technical Suggestions and Additional How-To's

trims and finishing techniques

How To Make Fringe

Cut strands of yarn double the length of fringe desired. Fold strands in half. Insert a crochet hook from front to back of edge of rug to be fringed; pull through the folded end of yarn strand (Fig. 1). Insert the two ends through loop (Fig. 2) and pull ends to tighten fringe. Repeat across edge with each doubled strand, placing strands close together or distance apart desired. For a fuller fringe, group a few strands together, and work as for one-strand fringe.

The fringe may be knotted after all strands are in place along edge. To knot, separate the ends of two adjacent fringes (or divide grouped fringes in half); hold together the adjacent ends and knot 1″ or more below edge (Fig. 3). Hold second end with one end of next fringe and knot together the same distance below edge as first knot. Continue across in this manner. A second row of knots may be made by separating the knotted ends again and knotting together the ends from two adjacent fringes in the same manner as for the first rows of knots.

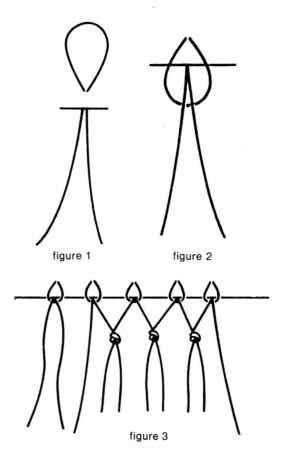

figure 1   figure 2

figure 3

HOW TO MAKE A FRINGE

Twisted Cord

Method requires two people. Tie one end of yarn around a pencil. Loop yarn over center of second pencil, then back to first, around first pencil and back to second, making as many strands between pencils as desired for thickness of cord. Knot end to pencil. Length of yarn between pencils should be three times length of cord desired. Each person holds yarn just below pencil with one hand and twists pencil with other hand, keeping yarn taut. When yarn begins to kink, catch center over a doorknob or hook. Bring pencils together for one person to hold while other grasps center of yarn, sliding hand down yarn and releasing it at short intervals, letting it twist.

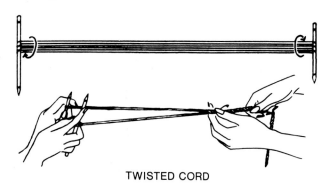

TWISTED CORD

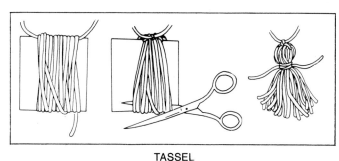

TASSEL

Tassels

Cut a piece of cardboard as wide as size of tassel desired. Wind yarn around cardboard 25 to 40 times, depending on thickness of yarn and plumpness of tassel required. Tie strands tightly together around top as shown, leaving at least 3″ ends on ties; clip other end of strands. Wrap piece of yarn tightly around strands a few times, about ½″ or 1″ below top tie and knot. Trim ends.

Finishing Edges
(Hand Hooking, Punch Needle)

The finished edge of a hooked rug must be planned before hooking is begun, or, if using a frame, before the foundation fabric is placed in the frame.

One method is to stitch 1¼″-wide rug binding at the edge of the rug design, on the front. The seam should be exactly on the edge of the rug, with the seam allowance of the binding and backing extending beyond. When hooking is completed, trim foundation to ½″, turn binding over edge of foundation, and slip-stitch to back of rug.

Another method is to trim the foundation to 2″ when hooking is completed. Fold margin in half, to underside; fold again to back of rug, and slip-stitch in place. Line entire rug with heavy cotton fabric.

A third method: Stitch rug binding at the edge of rug design as described above. Trim foundation to 1″ and fold to back; press and slip-stitch in place. If using a frame, attach foundation through binding. Hook through double thickness to outer edge, then turn binding to back of rug and slip-stitch in place.

Fringing Warp Cloth: If the foundation fabric is warp cloth rather than burlap, the rug can be fringed at the ends. Before starting to hook, pull several threads along selvage edge. Using the threads and a darning needle, work buttonhole stitch in each mesh along outside of line of pattern, working over three threads outside of line. This eliminates hemming and prevents raveling. When hooking is finished, cut warp cloth three to four inches from buttonholing and ravel the cross threads. On long sides of rug, cut off warp cloth along buttonholing.

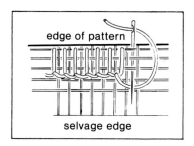

edge of pattern

selvage edge

FRINGING WARP CLOTH

Plaited Edge Stitch
(Needlepoint, Latch Hook)

Working from right to left, insert needle from back to front in first mesh of doubled canvas, leaving yarn end at top; bring needle from back to front in first mesh to left, under thread end (Fig. 1). Bring yarn over top; insert needle in first mesh again (Fig. 2).

Insert needle from back to front in third mesh to left (Fig. 3). Bringing yarn over top, insert needle back into second mesh to right from back to front (Fig. 4). Repeat Figs. 3 and 4 for edge.

When approaching the corners, shorten the stitch to cover the corner with a cross-stitch, as in Fig. 2. Work a short stitch twice in the corner.

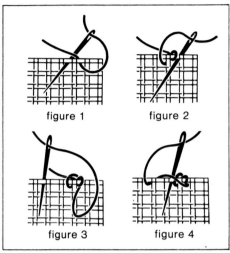

figure 1   figure 2

figure 3   figure 4

PLAITED EDGE STITCH

JOINING CANVAS
(Needlepoint, Latch Hook)

It is not always convenient to work a large latch-(latchet) hook or needlepoint rug on one piece of canvas. If working in sections, be sure to use canvas of the same mesh and weight for all pieces. Plan to work five rows over the joined sections; if using a chart, mark chart with parallel lines enclosing the five rows. Start work for each section 2" from edge to be joined. (If working in needlepoint, block each piece separately after it has been worked.) To join, carefully cut away all but four rows of unworked mesh on one of the two edges to be joined. Lap cut edge over corresponding edge so that the four rows of meshes on top coincide with the four rows of meshes below. Be sure both sides of both pieces line up correctly, matching warp (vertical) and weft (horizontal) threads. Pin pieces together, with large needles or pins, through center of lapped edges. Following pattern, work five rows over double thickness of canvas.

If a canvas thread is weak or has been accidentally cut, it is advisable to patch the area. Cut a piece of matching canvas ½" larger than the weak spot. Baste the patch to the wrong side of the canvas with matching wool, aligning the mesh of the two pieces. Continue working in pattern, stitching through both layers of canvas. Trim away ends of any canvas threads showing through.

rug frames
(needlepoint, hooked rugs)

Although the use of a rug frame is not absolutely required for hand-hooked or needlepoint rugs, many rugmakers find that the work is easier and their stitches are smoother with a frame. Canvas rugs worked in complicated stitches often require the use of a free hand under the canvas. A frame is always used when working with a punch needle, as the foundation fabric must be taut. There are several types of frames suitable for working hand-hooked, punch-needle, or needlepoint rugs. Three of these are illustrated on next page. The frame preferred for rugs is rectangular. Large round and oval frames are also used; however, they are not good for canvas work, as the frame may stretch the canvas out of shape.

The standing, easel-type frame is probably the most convenient to use. The easel frame tilts at any desired angle and can be revolved to reveal the underside for inspection; it stands at the usual table height of 30". Usually these frames have adjustable roller bars at top and bottom that make it easy to turn the foundation material in order to work on one part of the design at a time, rolling up the finished work as it is completed. The roller bars are attached to the side pieces in various ways: the simplest ones use pegs; others use clamps or screws for tightening and have ratchets to avoid slippage.

The foundation is attached to the roller bars, usually by basting through a strip of firm fabric (called listing or webbing) that has been thumbtacked or stapled to each roller bar. Or strips of sheeting may be tacked to each bar and wound around to make a firm padding; sew on foundation with close but loose stitches. First, machine-stitch raw edges if foundation is a fabric that tends to ravel. Find the center of both foundation and bar and sew from the centers out, following the same thread across. It is important that the foundation be straight in the frame before work is begun.

The foundation is also attached to the side bars of the frame. You can buy lacing sets, or you can devise your own by lacing heavy twine back and forth, sewing through the foundation and winding around the side bars or through holes drilled in the side bars or around ½" tacks. To keep the foundation from stretching out in peaks at the sides, run a knitting needle in and out along the edge and wind the string around the needle, or use straight pins set closely together along the edge. The strings will be untied and reset when the foundation is rolled to a new area. If the foundation is wider than the frame, attach foundation directly to the frame with ½" thumbtacks; make a ½" tuck in foundation on each side and tack to sides through tucks to reduce the strain.

Some may prefer table-model folding frames or lap frames. Lap frames are braced against the side of a chair, against a table, or attached to a table with a C clamp. These frames have the advantaje of being more portable than the standing models and are therefore useful for working on away from home.

To make a simple rug frame, glue and nail four strips of pine or softwood together and brace the inside corners with metal angles. To improvise a frame, try using one of the following: a picture frame, window screen, card table with the inside top removed, bassinet stand, stretcher bars for a painter's canvas, or weaver's loom with harnesses removed.

To make an adjustable frame, cut two 4-ft. crosspieces and two 1½-ft. sidepieces, using 1″ x 2″ lumber. Bore ½″ diameter holes at 3″ intervals on the side- and crosspieces; use wooden pegs in holes to adjust the size of the frame. The remaining side holes can be used for lacing on foundation.

designing rugs

CHOOSING A DESIGN

The choosing or planning of a design for a handmade rug is one of the best opportunities to express individuality. There are many rug-design influences from which to pick, ranging from the well-loved traditional patterns to the stimulating abstractions of modern artists.

Whether you are making your own original design or using one already available, size, shape, design style, and color should be considered in relation to where the rug is to be placed and the amount of wear it will receive.

Although you may wish to make a small rug for your first project, be sure the size and shape are correct for the area where the rug is to be used. We suggest that you cut a paper pattern of the estimated size from wrapping paper and leave it on the floor for a day or two; at the same time, plan the colors by placing a variety of fabric scraps on the paper pattern.

Think about the size, color, and design in relation to the other furnishings, attempting to keep not only a harmony of color but also of design motifs. Remember that in successful decorating, all of the items and the design motifs are related to each other in scale. Traditional and contemporary furnishings often combine well when all of the pieces have a related size and design style in accordance with their function.

Once the size of the rug is determined, be sure that the design you are planning is right for the size of your rug. Although repeat patterns can be used for almost any size rug, other types of designs must be planned so that the motifs are carefully arranged in relation to the background area. Study existing rug patterns such as the "Damask Rose Rug" on page 3, to see how shapes are arranged in space. The proportions of a design can be thrown off balance if the background is enlarged or decreased to achieve a desired size.

Most rug designs can be viewed from all angles. But a one-way design is attractive when used as a hearth rug, a welcome mat, or when it is to be viewed from only one side.

For large rugs in heavily traveled areas, choose medium shades, as they are the easiest to live with and show the least dirt. Brighter colors are used best in areas with few furnishings and poor light, such as hallways.

Plan the colors of the details in relation to each other. Use the brightest colors for the smallest details, and duller colors for large areas. Repeat colors over and over, especially if there is a great amount of detail, to give unity to the whole. A rug should "lie flat" on the floor. The rug design should be seen as a whole unit; no one motif or color should stand out to the extent that the eye is drawn to that area. For more about designing, see "Where to Find a Design," below.

Where to Find a Design

Take your inspiration from something purely personal—a favorite picture in your home, your pet, a pictorial representation of your hobby, a sampler of daily activities. Or work out a design inspired by your decor—repeat a motif taken from your wallpaper or draperies. Use colors of your decorating scheme.

Change the size or proportion to suit your needs and to fit the rug you plan to make. You can enlarge a small design for a bold, contemporary effect or reduce a large one to repeat for an allover pattern.

Research designs—look up and copy old designs from art books in your library or study actual pieces in museums. Use them as shown or vary designs to suit your own taste. Usually illustrations have been reduced from the size of the original; perhaps your library or museum has a photostating service, so that you can get the design you want to use blown up to full size. If not, with the permission of the library, place tracing paper over the photograph of the design and carefully copy the complete design; to protect the print, place a piece of glassine between the design and the tracing paper. Mark the correct colors and shades, using colored crayons or pencils. Then enlarge design by squares at home (see "Enlarging or Reducing Designs" on page 168).

TRANSFERRING DESIGNS TO RUG FOUNDATION

If you are creating your own rug design, you will need to mark a pattern on the foundation material; burlap or warp cloth is used for hand hooking and punch needle, rug canvas for latch (latchet) hooking and needlepoint. (Exception: The pattern is not marked on the foundation if a chart is being used to work a canvas pattern.)

Before marking the design, the fabric or canvas must be spread out flat on a large table or on the floor. Weight the edges with heavy objects—irons, large books, etc.—to keep the material taut, with the threads straight and true; or you can secure the material with thumbtacks if working on a soft, unfinished wooden surface.

Before placing the design, mark the overall size and shape of the rug. When planning the placement of design elements, mark center lines vertically and horizontally with a soft pencil, in order to be able to center the main motif and arrange the border in a pleasing fashion.

Designs on Burlap or Warp Cloth: There are several methods of marking a design on fabric. Some straight-line designs can be drawn directly on the foundation—for example, the Shaded Tile Rug on page 20.

A simple way of transferring a design is to make a tracing and mark it on the fabric, using carbon paper. If design is to be worked with a hand hook, trace it as given on right side of fabric. If design is to be worked with a punch needle and is not symmetrical, it should be reversed when traced on wrong side of fabric.

Place carbon face down on fabric; lay tracing over carbon; tape in place. With a blunt point, such as the tip of a knitting needle, trace around the outlines of the large areas within the motifs, leaving the color shading details to be worked out as you hook. To remove loose carbon, lay paper towels over design and press with hot iron.

A design may also be transferred to fabric by going over all lines on back of tracing with a soft pencil. Then tape tracing onto your fabric, right side up, and trace all lines again, using a hard pencil.

If there are large leaves, scallops, bird or flower shapes, you may find it easier to cut the shapes out of stiff wrapping paper; these may then be laid on the foundation and drawn around. To make a symmetrical design, flop the paper shape and draw it in reverse. Colorfast grease pencils, felt-tipped marking pens, or crayons are excellent to use for drawing designs. If using a wax crayon, cover completed design with paper towels and go over design with a hot iron to set lines and remove excess wax.

Two other methods of transferring designs are described under the sections "Perforated Pattern" and "Painting in the Design" (below).

Designs on Canvas: Patterns for canvas-based rugs may be marked directly on the canvas or worked out in chart form on graph paper.

To make a chart, use each square of graph paper to represent one stitch on the canvas, using symbols to indicate colors. Or instead of marking symbols in each square, you can color the areas of the design on the graph paper. In working out the design, be sure you have the same number of squares on the graph paper as there are meshes within the rug area of the canvas. To do this, you will probably have to piece together the sheets of graph paper. Follow the chart, using each square to represent one mesh of canvas, working in latch-(latchet) hook knots or needlepoint stitches.

A method of copying a design is to rule lines representing canvas threads over the design, scaled to exact size of finished piece. If necessary, enlarge or reduce design (see page 168) before ruling lines.

To mark a design on canvas directly, first trace the design on paper in actual size in a heavy black outline, using India ink and a pointed paintbrush. Place design under the canvas; the heavy outlines will be visible through the canvas mesh. In using this method, paint curved outlines as curves on the canvas; do not attempt to indicate each individual stitch. Plan placement of individual stitches on curves while working latch (latchet) hook or needlepoint.

Perforated Pattern: This method of transferring designs may be used for burlap and warp-cloth foundations as well as canvas. In many large cities it is possible to have a perforated pattern made professionally from your tracing. Look for such a company under Perforated Patterns in the classified phone directory. To make your own perforated pattern, mark design accurately on a large sheet of heavy-quality tracing paper or wrapping paper. Then perforate the traced design on all outlines, using the longest stitch on the sewing machine and no thread in the needle; stitch through all lines of the design. If a sewing machine is not available, place tracing on a lightly padded surface and make holes through lines with a large pin, about 1/16″ apart; hold the pin straight up and push through paper enough to make clear holes. When the perforating is finished, place pattern over your fabric, smooth side up, and weight or tape it down around edges to hold in place while transferring. The design may be transferred by means of a perforating paste and a pounce. To make a pounce, roll up a strip of flannel or felt tightly, sewing it so it remains rolled. Dip pounce in benzene, rub the end of the pounce in the paste, then dab and rub it over the perforated outlines. Carefully lift up a corner of perforated pattern to see if design has been transferred clearly. If not, go over it again with the pounce. When transferring is completed, carefully lift off pattern.

Painting in the Design: The easiest method for the rugmaker to follow is to have the design painted on the foundation, with various areas colored to correspond to the wool colors to be used. Designs may be painted on burlap and warp-cloth foundations as well as canvas, if you are careful to use a thin paint solution to keep from clogging the fabric. For a simple design with few colors, color areas can be filled in with wax crayons, grease pencils, or felt-tipped marking pens. If a wax crayon is used, cover completed design with paper towels and go over with a hot iron to set design and remove excess wax.

For complex designs, painting a design on fabric or canvas with oil paints is not difficult. Use inexpensive tube oils. Buy the following colors: white, lemon yellow, cadium yellow light, yellow ochre, vermilion, alizarin crimson, ultramarine blue, viridian green, Vandyke brown, burnt sienna, black. With these colors, desired shades can be mixed to match the yarns.

The foundation to be painted is stretched tightly on a board over a piece of brown paper to absorb oil. Colors are mixed and then thinned to consistency of light cream with a clear liquid cleaning fluid having a naphtha or benzene base. This cuts oil and keeps colors from spreading; it makes paint dry quickly. Skill is required to learn how to mix exact consistency of paint so that it is not so thin it changes color and not so thick it clogs the canvas.

Some colors—black, for instance—have a tendency to take a long time to dry. If this is the case, add a tiny bit of Japan drier. Usually, oil paint thinned with cleaning fluid alone will dry overnight.

Use soft, pointed brushes for painting. Japanese watercolor brushes are very good for this purpose; they hold quite a bit of paint and have a good point. Wash brushes frequently with turpentine.

dyeing fabrics
(braided, hand-hooked rugs)

It is not difficult to dye fabrics for braided and hand-hooked rugs. Follow the directions given on the dye package, but do not worry about getting an even tone if fabric is to be used for hooking, as variations in shading give depth and character to the design of a hooked rug.

Fabrics in white or light colors can easily be dyed a darker shade. If you wish to dye a dark material a lighter shade, however, first remove the color.

To dye several shades of one color, start by making enough dye for all the shades. (Prepare more dye than you think you need; it is better to have too much than not enough, because it will be almost impossible later to match colors exactly.) Dye material about two shades darker when wet than the desired color. Make the color you want for the darkest shade; dye this shade first, remove fabric, then put into the same dye mixture the fabric for the next lighter shade, etc. As each piece absorbs some of the color, the next piece will be a bit lighter.

To shade fabric that is already cut into strips, hold five strips at one end and dip the other end in the dye for five minutes. Reverse the ends and hold in dye for three minutes; hold both ends and dip center in the dye for one minute.

For a mottled effect rather than even shading, wet the material to be dyed, wring it out, and spread out flat on a newspaper. With a teaspoon, drop blotches of dye on the material. Roll up tightly; unroll when dry.

For mottling strips, tie a few together in several knots and drop into the dye. Untie when dry.

After fabric is dyed, each color should be washed in warm water with borax or naphtha soap, rinsed without wringing, and hung in sunlight to dry. This helps to make the rug more washable and colorfast.

how to draw an oval

Here is the simple geometrical method of making ovals large or small to fit any desired space.

Fig. 1: Draw a straight line length of, or longer than, desired length of oval. At center of line establish point A. With compass (or pencil tied to string) swing arcs to establish B and C, the length of oval.

Fig. 2: From B and C swing arcs above and below line BC. Connect their intersections with line DE. On this line mark points F and G equal distances from A, to establish width of oval.

Fig. 3: Mark points 1 and 2 to match A and C on a straight, firm strip of paper.

Fig. 4: Turn this measuring paper vertically along line FG so that point 1 is at F. Mark point 3 at A.

Fig. 5: Rotate the measuring paper clockwise, moving point 3 along line AC and point 2 along AG. Make dots opposite point 1. Connect these dots with a line which completes the first quarter of the oval. Repeat this procedure in the other three parts or make a tracing and transfer curve to complete oval.

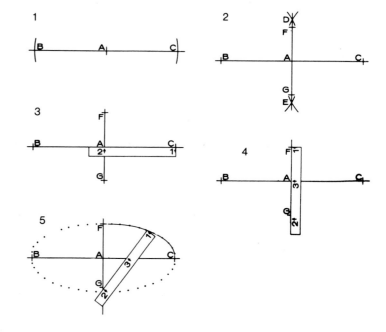

how to divide any line into equal parts

Fig. 1: The line to be divided will be called line X. Rule off line AB shorter than line X by marking off AB into the desired number of equal parts, using simple divisions on ruler such as ½", ¼", etc.

Fig. 2: With a draftsman's triangle, or holding an ordinary ruler at right angles to line AB, raise perpendicular lines at each division.

Fig. 3: Measure line X and mark off length on ruler. Place ruler so that line X extends from A to line BC; where it touches is point D. Line X is now divided into equal parts.

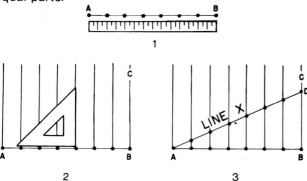

how to make a star

1. Draw a circle desired size of star. With compass or dividers, find five equidistant points A on circumference of circle. Draw lines to connect points to form a pentagon.

2. Using same center of circle, draw another circle inside larger circle as illustrated (distance of inner circle from outer circle controls depth of star points). Find centers of five sides of pentagon (points B). From these centers, draw lines through center of circle to opposite points A.

3. Draw lines from points A of pentagon to where dividing lines intersect inner circle (points C).

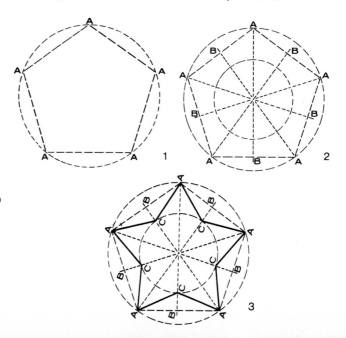

enlarging or reducing designs

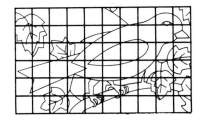

There are various ways of enlarging or reducing a design so that all parts of the design will be enlarged or reduced in proportion. Two methods are given here. The most commonly used is the "square" method, No. 1. Another simple procedure is the "diagonal" method, No. 2.

If you wish to keep the original design unmarked, trace the outlines onto tracing paper.

Method No. 1: Mark off squares over the design to be enlarged. Use 1/8" squares for small designs and 1/4", 1/2", or 1" squares for proportionately larger designs. Make the same number of squares, similarly placed, in the space to be occupied by the enlarged design. Copy the outline of design from the smaller squares to the corresponding larger squares. Reverse the procedure for reducing designs.

Method No. 2: Make a rectangle to fit around design to be enlarged. Draw a diagonal line from corner to corner and extend line far enough to form diagonal of a rectangle to fit desired size.

Subdivide large and small rectangles by first making opposite diagonals to find center. Then draw lines to quarter the space. Make diagonal of quarter sections to find centers. Draw lines to quarter the space. Copy the outlines of design from smaller areas to larger areas or vice versa. An easy way to divide the rectangles into spaces described above is to fold the paper into halves, quarters, and eighths, then draw diagonal lines into folds.

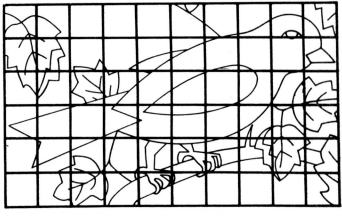

Method No. 1: A bird drawing enlarged on squares

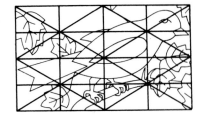

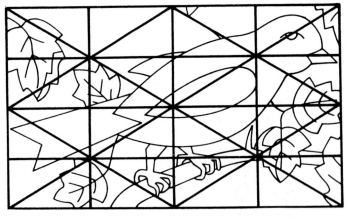

Method No. 2: Enlarging bird drawing on diagonals